Microfuture

John Shelley

MPhil, DIC, MBCS

Pitman

Contents

This book is dedicated to Rosalind and Mari-Elena to compensate for the many lost weekends and evenings

PITMAN EDUCATION LIMITED
39 Parker Street, London WC2B 5PB

Associated Companies
Pitman Publishing New Zealand Ltd, Wellington
Pitman Publishing Pty Ltd, Melbourne

© J Shelley 1981

First published in Great Britain 1981

ISBN 0 273 01676 8

Preface

Electronic devices are nothing new. They abound in many products which we take for granted, especially in domestic entertainment in our radios, television sets, music centres and video-tape recorders. What is new is *microelectronics*.

The crucial difference between yesterday's electronic products and today's microelectronic devices is that the latter contain computers, thus turning them into devices which contain a degree of intelligence. Many benefits accrue from this single feature but there are some potential dangers.

This book will not provide a technical study of microelectronics, too many texts already exist. Instead, we consider the nature of microprocessors and microcomputers; where they came from, how they are related to the traditional computer; their benefits as well as potential problems; how they are used; and their implications for society and the world at large.

In the preparation of this text I am grateful to the following for their contributions: Dr Alexander Forti, Toshiba, National Semiconductors, Intel Corporation, Research Machines of Oxford, Central Office of Information, Tektronix, Monsanto, Ferranti, UniChem, E & L Instruments (UK), IBM (UK), Microsystem Services, Phil Goodman and John Cushion of Pitmans.

Text set in 10/12 pt Linotron 202 Century, printed and bound in Great Britain at The Pitman Press, Bath

One
Why We Need to Know About Microcomputers

Microprocessors have arrived and they are here to stay no matter what we as individuals may feel about them. What is more, the world will never be quite the same again. Ten years ago, 99.9% of the population had never heard about them; today it would be difficult to find anyone in industrial societies who has not heard of them. Already, such domestic products as ovens, microwave ovens, sewing machines, washing machines, cameras and television games are controlled by microprocessors. They appear in learning aids, petrol pumps, taximeters. Some entire factories are automated via these devices. Before long, they will teach our children, and become widespread in small businesses, shops and the professions. Even now they can be embedded in the human heart to control the rate at which an artificial pacemaker should beat; and be used by severely handicapped people to control the movement of artificial limbs; and can even speak for people with impaired larynx.

The *electronic age* is just beginning to flower. Within a few years, perhaps even a decade, we could see the demise of paper and metal money in exchange for electronic money; the decline of the printed book as electronic books flood the market; the end of our traditional postal service as electronic mail becomes more widely used; we shall even throw away our old front-door keys and replace them with electronic locks which open to the sound of our voices and unique finger-prints. Cars will not skid or crash or even operate if the driver has been drinking. Health devices worn on the wrist will have sensors reading our pulses, monitoring our temperatures, assessing our skin moisture, and analysing the surrounding atmosphere for viruses. What is more, we shall be able to communicate with micros in the way we communicate with each other, by voice, gestures and touch.

Microprocessors promise many benefits, yet there will be disadvantages too. In this book, the microprocessor is examined in some detail. It is placed in relationship to the traditional computer, now some thirty years old. We shall discuss why we need microprocessors, what they are, where they have come from, and how they will be used. We shall also see how they will affect our societies and become a force in world politics. However, before we become too absorbed in the future, let us for the moment begin with the present time.

The present

The Western World is *already* deeply committed to computers in their traditional form. Were all computers to be made to vanish overnight, the financial empires of the West would collapse, affecting not only financial professionals but every adult and child. Just think about it – no bank cheques could be passed, no credit cards used, no social security payments made, no wages, salaries or insurance premiums paid, no business transactions made, and so on.

As we shall see, computers are primarily handlers of information, and financial data is only one aspect of information in general. Consequently, many other areas of our society would be affected by the overnight demise of the computer. Companies with computerised stock control, invoicing and other commercial activities, hospital records, the telephone system, airline reservations, air traffic control, space exploration, would have to cease. We are therefore heavily committed to computers; the microprocessor will ensure that this trend continues.

Furthermore, computers are far too convenient to be given up. Mankind is always searching for something new and, when it is found, it is not relinquished lightly. There are too many precedents for us to doubt this: the industrial revolution, electricity, the motor car, the pocket calculator. We want the computer and we are going to keep it. It is going to fulfil some of mankind's as yet unrealised ambitions and we are not going to sacrifice that opportunity, it is not in our nature to do so.

But why do we need computing power? Although this is discussed more fully in the next chapter, for the moment we can state that computers are needed because they assist man with handling *information*. It is strange then that the Concise Oxford Dictionary (sixth edition, 1976) should call a computer "a reckoner, calculator; automatic electronic apparatus for making calculations or controlling operations that are expressible in numerical or logical terms". Today this emphasis on calculation is misplaced. It is true that the early prototype computers were used exclusively as calculating devices but it was soon appreciated that computers were capable of *storing* information in what is called a "memory" or "store". Without this ability to hold pre-recorded information on a vast scale, computers would never have succeeded.

The commercial world then became interested, so much so that today 80% of computer applications are related to commercial information rather than mathematical information. Therefore, a more accurate definition of a computer is that it is a **processor of information**; that is, it can receive our everyday information (provided that it has been encoded into a computer-readable format), perform manipulations on that information, and reproduce results for our convenience

The microprocessor fits into this overall picture by being a computer, yet smaller and cheaper than the traditional computer. A few years ago, computerisation of many applications, although feasible, would have been too expensive. Today, for the same applications, the microprocessor can be used because the price has tumbled so low as to be within the reach indeed of the man-in-the-street. For example, five to ten years ago a computer of modest size (the minicomputer) would have cost £50 000, too much for the average estate agent, general practitioner, surveyor or school. Today the equivalent computer power can be purchased for under £4000 in the form of a microcomputer.

What this means is that many professions, trades, individuals, and areas of society, which could not afford to think about computing power, can now afford to do so. But what is more important, is that very soon people from all walks of life will not be able to afford *not* to think about computer power.

The 1980s

During the early 1980s microprocessors will become much more widespread. The motor car industry is beginning to use them to reduce fuel consumption and air pollution. More sophisticated microcomputers are being used in hundreds of secondary and tertiary level educational establishments. Systems are being offered to general practitioners to perform the complicated National Health payment system. Estate agents are being offered systems which will produce their mailing lists.

Speech synthesis has already been successful in some electronic learning aids such as "Speak & Spell" (already popular in the USA and just becoming known in the UK). The aid will pronounce letters and words and short sentences very clearly and complete with voice inflection. This latter development will soon find its way into speaking bathroom scales (not a gimmick if you are poorly sighted or your tummy is too big to let you read the scales). Cookers will tell you when the roast is ready or when to put on the potatoes and vegetables. Our freezers will tell us when to defrost and re-stock. Our telephones will tell us how many calls were received in our absence, who called, when they called, and when to call back (not quite the same as ansaphone since pre-recorded messages could be left for certain callers). Doorbells, apart from choosing between twenty-four different chimes, will let us know how many visitors called and when they called. Already, speaking calculators are being marketed (very useful if you are blind or if you do not want to take your eyes away from your figures, or, as an airline pilot, you do not want to look away from the instrument panel). Our future motor cars will have talking controls, headlights will come on automatically when daylight falls below a certain level, and keep a safe distance from other vehicles in front.

Many of these features are pure gimmicks, yet people adore them. Watch the proud face of an owner of a bleeping watch demonstrating his little device and his triumphant grin when it bleeps. An excited friend of mine could not wait to show me the calculator/watch/calendar device his wife bought him for Christmas. However, an important point about all these gadgets and gimmicks is that the real impact of microprocessors will ride in on their backs. The profits they make will be ploughed back into more research and development for more sophisticated devices so that the 1980s will see the growth of a vast new industry, rising perhaps to the number one spot of the world's largest companies, currently held by General Motors. The 1970s saw the giant computer company IBM rise to number seven.

More sophisticated devices

A limiting factor of current calculator-type devices is the size of the key or button necessary to input numerical information. Once *voice recognition* devices can be made small enough to fit into wristwatches and calculators, these keys will become largely redundant. We shall be able to speak to our calculators and they will display our utterances as a check that they have "heard" correctly and then display the results. Display devices will also include alphabetic characters as well as numeric, and then our wristwatch will become our personal notebook holding telephone numbers, names and addresses, as well as other reminders. If a TV scanner is added to our lawn mower then it can be told when and how to cut the grass; and our motor car can tell us when it is due for a service.

Towards 2000

Whilst we are absorbed in this general seduction by electronic gadgets, the microprocessor will be establishing itself as the number one industry and Japan as the number one computer nation. The Japanese government has invested many thousands of millions of dollars into their microcomputer industry and this investment will begin to pay for itself during the 1980s.

During the 1990s industrial societies will become as dependent upon computer power as today they are upon the telephone and electricity. Those societies without computer power will become less and less effective and more and more dependent upon those which have.

It is inevitable within the next decade or two, and certainly during the lifetimes of our children, that economic and political decisions of immense importance will be based upon information produced by computers. What is more intriguing, however, is that no one person or, indeed, group of persons will be able to challenge this information. The original information or data from which the computer gleans its results may be challenged; the decisions made by economists and politicians may be challenged; but not the information produced by the computer. Bureaucracies will become more reliant upon the computer in order to sift through the ever-increasing amount of information which is rapidly becoming too much for the unaided mind.

But what about the so-called Third World which has already missed out on the traditional computer technology? Is the technology gap going to widen even more with microprocessors? Strangely enough, the microprocessor may be the very technology to bridge this gap.

A changed world

As the year 2000 looms nearer, and it is only 20 years away, our world will have changed. Electronic devices will control many manufacturing processes, such as paint spraying, welding, and component assembly. Even the plough-boy on the land will be replaced by robot-controlled tractors. Medical screening and diagnoses, routine teaching of our children, preparing judgements in certain legal cases, all these and more will be performed as routine by computers. Educating the public about these computers will have been achieved long before, since, even today, a substantial number of children are exposed to computers whilst at school. Some 37 000 children entered CSE and GCE computer examinations in 1980; and thus a generation is growing up which will have some real understanding about computing. Electronic books will be much cheaper than our present-day books; thus education will become cheaper.

It is here that the Third World may begin to benefit from microprocessor technology. The advances in electronic mail, which will allow information to pass via satellite communications to any part of the world at speeds approaching that of light, will permit underdeveloped countries to access stores of learning and knowledge held in memory chips capable of storing not just a book but whole libraries. Furthermore these electronic books will not passively hold information, as does this book which you are reading, but will actively teach its contents to its reader. Ignorance is probably the chief obstacle to development for the Third World; microprocessors have the means to eliminate this obstacle permanently.

If this is not enough in the way of change, there is much more yet to come. Man has had many dreams, to fly, to travel faster than animals, to land on the moon, to explore space, to create intelligent machines. Most of these he has already achieved with the help of technology. The microprocessor can help him to achieve the last. Part of the reason is our need to do so. Societies of the world have to face increasingly complex problems which are gradually becoming too complex for the unaided human mind to solve. We need assistance in the form of intelligent machines. A little headway has been made so far, but the 1990s will show a great determination to extend our present understanding of *machine intelligence* (or *artificial intelligence* as it is sometimes called). In time, these machines may well acquire an intelligence far greater than our own. Such *ultra intelligent machines* (UIMs) may appear fanciful, but already certain computer scientists (e.g. J. Weizenbaum) of exceptional ability are calling for a halt into artificial intelligence because of the unknown dangers and threat to man himself.

Two
The Traditional Computer

The image of computers presented by television and cinema gives the impression that they are very advanced, such as the lovable little canine (K9) in the BBC's Doctor Who series and the friendly but eventually frightening Hal from the film 2001, or, if presented as machines of today, they are depicted as consisting of winking lights, moving tapes and punched cards. Both are false images. In this chapter, we shall present the computer as it really is and see that it is a much more mundane piece of technology.

Currently, electronics provide the most convenient technology for constructing computers. It is not surprising, therefore, that electronic circuits form the basic unit. Such circuits are more easily manufactured (and thus cheaper) as **two-state devices**, rather like the domestic light bulb which can be in one of only two possible states at any given time, i.e. either on or off but never half way. A two-state electronic circuit is capable of conducting an electrical signal at one time or not conducting one at another time. However, computer people tend not to talk about the presence or absence of signals, preferring instead to use some other representation. An ideal system to represent the two possible states is the binary or base-two number system since it possesses only two digits, zero and one (0,1). It is for this reason that the binary digits (often shortened to **bits**) are associated with computers. We tend to assume that internally the computer contains thousands of bits (zeros and ones) although, strictly speaking, computers contain only electrical signals.

Communicating with a computer

Languages exist to convey information. The natural language of a computer is electrical signals which we prefer to represent as bits. Thus, information inside a computer can be said to consist of binary digits. Yet our everyday written information is different and is coded into symbols which you are reading now: namely, letters of the alphabet, the decimal digits (zero through to nine, 0–9), punctuation symbols, and other symbols which express mathematical and scientific concepts (for example, +, −, × and ÷). Human beings then have a problem when communicating with computing machines. Some of the first computer designers who were also the programmers argued that, since binary was the natural language of the computer, then the human being had to communicate with it via binary. Fortunately, this point of view was a temporary one because binary communication proves to be most tedious and unnatural for humans. Devices were constructed which were capable of translating our everyday characters into binary information and passing it into the computers (figure 2.1). Thus, **input devices** are required to enter information into computers.

There are various types of input devices. *Card readers* are designed to read information which has been punched as patterns or combinations of holes on a punched card (see figure 2.2). *Keyboard* devices, somewhat similar to electric typewriters but called **terminal** devices, translate into binary information the characters selected by the operator depressing the keys. In supermarkets we are already

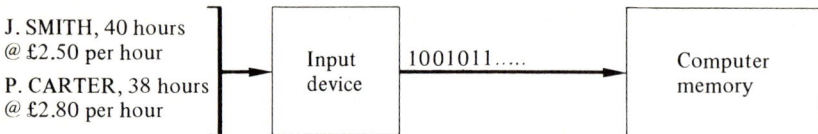

Figure 2.1 An input device converts our everyday characters into binary information which can then be passed into the memory of the computer.

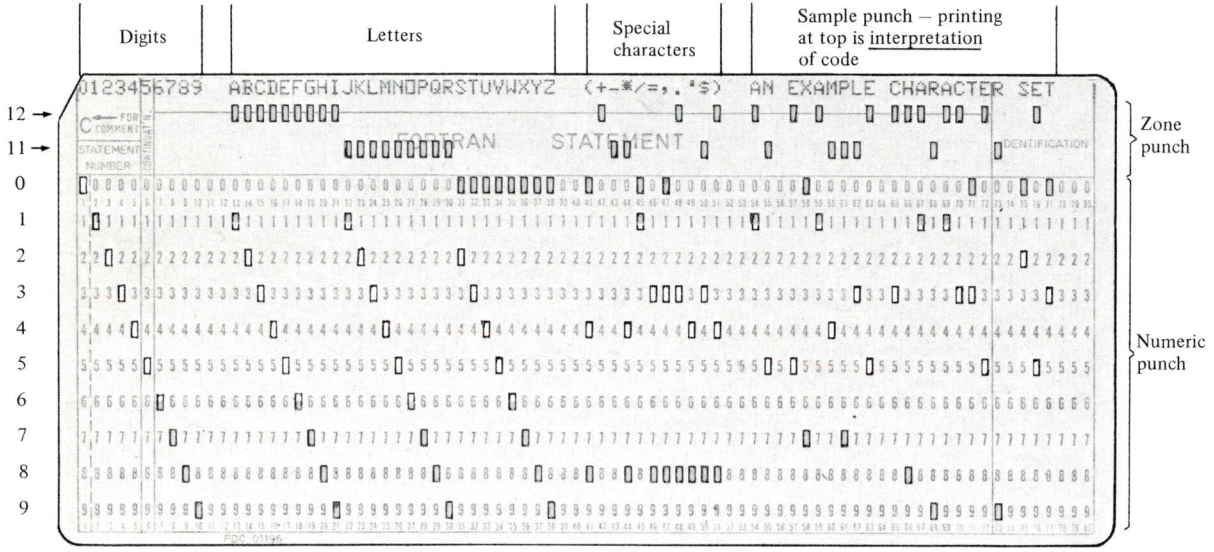

Each digit is represented by a single numeric punch.

Each letter is represented by a single zone punch and a single numeric punch.

Each symbol is represented by a combination of one, two or three punches (zone and/or numeric).

Figure 2.2 An 80-column punched card. Letters, numbers and special characters can be represented in any column by holes punched on the card according to the Hollerith code.

becoming accustomed to seeing wand readers (figure 2.3) reading information expressed as lines. Advances in voice recognition devices may enable us to talk more naturally to computers in the not too distant future.

The information entered into the computer frequently needs to be processed or manipulated according to a set of previously defined instructions (a computer program) to produce results. However, these results are *inside* the computer as a series of binary digits. There is

no way of opening the computer in order to see these results and, consequently, some other piece of machinery is required which can re-translate binary digits into human-readable characters. The device which performs the opposite of an input machine is called an output device (see figure 2.4).

There are various types of **output device.** Printing machines can print on computer paper or on special forms such as payslips, telephone and electricity accounts, bank statements, etc.

Figure 2.3 A wand device used to input information into a computer memory. (*Courtesy: IBM UK Ltd.*)

Computers may also output information onto cathode ray tubes similar to television screens but called **visual display units** (VDUs). Specialised VDUs may permit graphs and designs to be displayed as well as text characters (see figure 2.5). If a copy of a graph or design is required permanently, this may be transferred to another device which can reproduce the design onto A4 size paper. This permanent copy on paper is referred to as a **hard copy** in contrast to the screen copy which will be lost when the VDU is switched off.

Of much greater impact are devices which can speak to us. This is still an area of research and development which is expected to become far more common within the next five years. These so-called *speech synthesis* devices are currently to be found in electronic toys such as "Speak & Spell" made by Texas Instruments, mentioned earlier, and are of surprising sophistication.

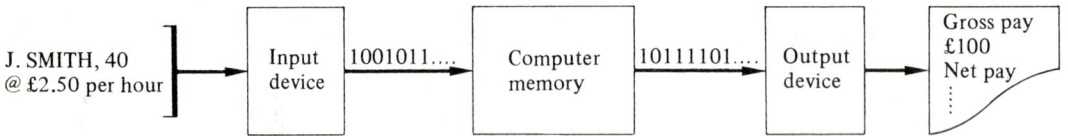

Figure 2.4 An output device re-converts binary information into a human-readable format.

Figure 2.5 A graphics terminal linked to another unit which can produce a hard copy of the screen information.
(*Courtesy*: *Tektronix*)

The computer

Soon we will turn our attention to the problem of how the two binary digits can be made to represent our many and varied everyday characters. But first we need to look and see what is inside the computer. Computers are used to help individuals or organisations, both small and large, with certain tasks. These tasks may be of a mathematical or scientific nature: such as weather forecasting; the control of laboratory or industrial equipment (process control),

as in the process of refining crude oil; or in processing commercial information (data processing) as in invoicing, stock control, insurance premiums, and payroll applications.

In order to perform any of these applications, for example calculating a given employee's payslip, what does a computer need? If we were to use a human colleague as opposed to a computer as an assistant, what would we have to give our colleague? First, some **instructions** either verbally or in written form so that he or she would know what to do. These would be retained in his or her memory. The next thing our colleague would want would be the specific information relating to that employee's work details, e.g. the number of hours worked, rate of pay per hour, tax code, etc. This information is more formally termed **data**, hence the term **data processing**.

A computer requires the same information – a set of instructions, called the **program,** and data. Both must be stored in the **memory** of the computer. Thus, we should expect to find a memory, for historical reasons frequently called a *store*, as a major component of a computer. But this store is used only to retain information (program instructions and data). No computation can take place in the store. Therefore, in order to calculate the "number of hours" times "rate per hour", a second component is required. This is called the **arithmetic unit** and is designed to perform any of the four basic arithmetic operations of addition, subtraction, multiplication, and division.

Now, a computer program will contain many instructions, maybe several hundreds or even thousands for a more complex application. These are held in the store where they remain passive. A third and final component must exist which can interpret and carry out the given computer instructions in a program, one at a time, until there are no more instructions left. This third component is called a **control unit**. It will select an instruction from memory according to a pre-determined order and not just at random, and take it into a special decoding circuit which is designed to understand and obey any program instruction.

For example, "calculate number of hours times rate per hour". This is step 1 in figure 2.6. The specific data for Joe Smith (40 hours at £2.50 per hour) is stored in the memory. Therefore, the control unit will have to take these data items from store and place them in the arithmetic unit (step 2). So far so good, but now the control unit must nudge the arithmetic unit to perform a multiplication operation (step 3) and, then, return the result (£100) as a fourth step to the memory unit.

The control unit (CU) then is like a master

unit controlling the processing of instructions and movement of data to the arithmetic unit (AU) and back to memory. This may seem complicated but in reality is no more complicated than a tap or a valve.

In figure 2.6, we have printed everyday characters inside the memory unit (purely for our own convenience) when, in reality, these characters will be represented as electrical signals. These signals are held in memory in a similar fashion to water held in a loft tank. When signals represent an instruction, valves open under the control of the CU to allow these to flow from memory into the control unit's decoder. If the signals represent an item of data, then valves (or more formally **gates** in electronic terminology) allow this item to flow from memory into the AU. If a result is produced, then the CU opens those gates which permit the signals to pass into the memory unit. The CU then is a master controller of gates, opening some and closing others at the right time. That is its whole function. The complexity lies in the precise timing of each step and in the opening of the correct gates, which typically run into many thousands and even millions in the very large computers.

The three components, the store, the arithmetic unit and the control unit, are collectively known as the **central processing unit**, or CPU for short. It is these units which comprise the computer as we know it today. No matter how large or small, how cheap or expensive, any computer consists only of these three units.

The computer store

The store of a computer can be likened to the honeycomb which consists of many sections, each of which stores or holds honey. In the case of the computer store, each section (called a **location** or **word**) can hold one program instruction, or one piece of data, or one result from some previous computation. The number of memory locations varies from manufacturer to manufacturer but are packaged in what are called 1K modules where K stands for the binary kilo, namely 1024. Thus, a computer

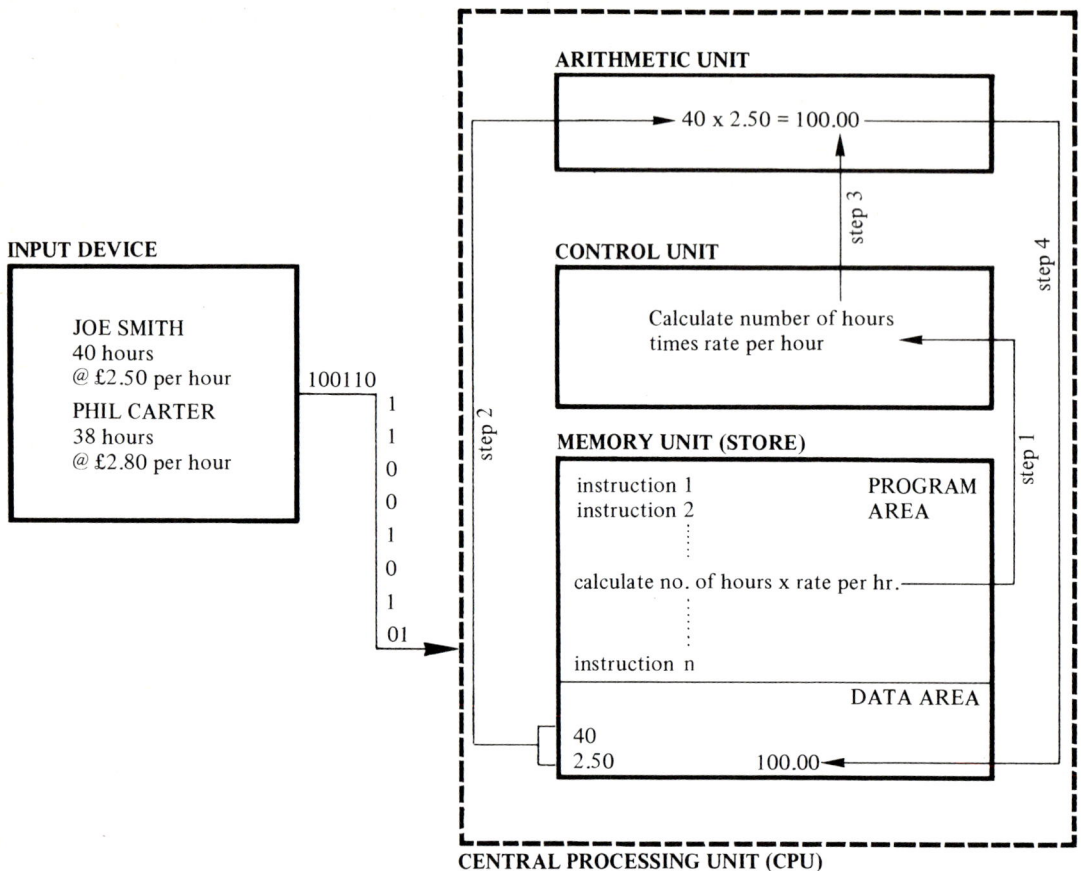

Figure 2.6 Four steps in obeying an instruction:

1 An instruction is taken into the Control Unit;
2 A copy of the data numbers (40, 2.50 in this case) are sent to the Arithmetic Unit;
3 The A.U. is ordered to perform multiplication on the two numbers;
4 Finally, the computed result (100) is sent to the memory unit.

with a 4K memory will have 4×1024, i.e. 4096 individual locations or words.

These locations are expensive and are therefore limited in number in order to reduce the overall cost of the computer. Yet in many applications, computers have to have access to many millions of data items. These cannot be contained in this limited store. Consequently, **auxiliary storage devices** are necessary. These are magnetic devices such as magnetic tapes and magnetic discs, and are familiar to anyone

who owns a music centre since they are very similar to music cassette tapes and records, except that, instead of music, they store binary digits. A typical magnetic tape of 2400 feet in length (larger versions of our music tapes) can store between 10 million and 40 million characters of text. Discs can contain more than 200 million characters. Several tapes and discs, therefore, can store a vast amount of data.

Information thus contained, however, is useless unless it is placed in the central store of the

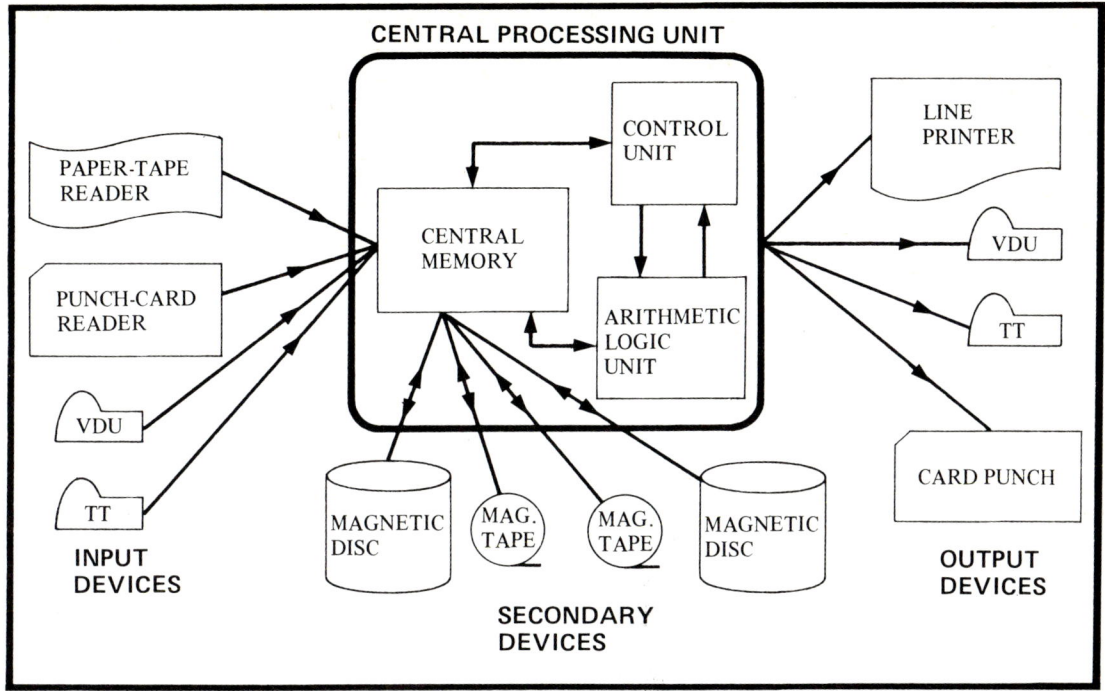

Figure 2.7 Computer system hardware.
(TT = teletype terminal, VDU = visual display unit)

computer, since the CPU can only be aware of what is inside its own central memory. Obviously, 10 million characters from a tape would swamp the limited capacity of the central store. Thus, information from tapes or discs has to be organised into much smaller units or blocks, so that each block can fit easily into the central memory. It will be part of a programmer's work to organise data in this fashion. When one block of binary information has been processed, then a second block can be read into the main memory for processing, and so on.

The computer system

We can now complete the basic design of a computer by adding in the auxiliary storage devices as in figure 2.7. The CPU is the real computer. Input devices are designed to get information as it exists in the outside world into a computer-readable format and to put that information into the main store. The output device is there to translate binary information held in the main store into a human-readable format (or even into a spoken format). The auxiliary storage devices hold vast quantities of data and programs permanently outside the CPU. This information can be accessed very quickly by the CPU, e.g. thousands of characters (i.e. this entire chapter) can pass into the central store within the space of one second. The input, output and magnetic auxiliary storage devices are therefore on the periphery of the CPU and, indeed, are frequently called **peripheral units**. These peripheral units and the three components of the CPU are those boxes or devices which can be seen and touched when touring a computer installation room. They are called **hardware** and will come in all different shapes and sizes and colours, depending on the imagination of the manufacturer.

However, the computer hardware by itself is

of little value, like a taxi-cab which by itself is nothing more than a useless piece of hardware. The taxi requires a taxi driver to turn its hardware into a functioning unit. Likewise for computer hardware. The individual units have to work as a functional whole in order to be of value. As with the taxi, they need a driver which is capable of making the various units function as a whole machine. "Driving programs" are required which collectively have the more formal title of **computer operating system software**. The term "software", then, applies to a set of programs which turn the hardware units into a working unit. However, a user of a computer requires another piece of software in order to perform useful tasks. These are called **application programs**, each of which will tell the functioning computer to perform a specific task, for example a payroll, guidance of an Apollo craft through space, traffic control at a specified junction.

These application programs can be related to the passenger in a taxi who wishes the driver to transport him in the hardware from one location to another.

To summarise, we can identify three separate elements in a computer system. First, there is the computer hardware system; secondly, the driving software which transforms the hardware units into a functional unit – the computer operating system software; and finally, the application programs which permit the computer system, i.e. both the hardware and the operating system, to perform some useful task.

Encoding

Human thought has been encoded in many different ways. For example, in the form of braille a blind person can "read" the thoughts of another; combinations of six dots can be made to represent the characters used by sighted people. Combinations of dots and dashes are used to transmit information to someone who can understand Morse code. The shorthand secretary represents thoughts and words in shorthand hieroglyphics. English-speaking

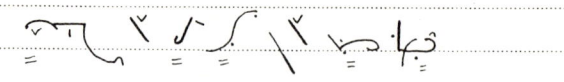

Figure 2.8 An example of Pitman shorthand.

people can understand the Roman alphabet but, for those who do not understand the Cyrillic alphabet, the Russian language would prove impossible to understand. We are accustomed therefore to representing our ideas in a variety of ways. Why should binary digits present any more difficulty?

The English alphabet consisting of 26 letters and the ten digits, zero through to nine, make 36 characters in all. But even when special punctuation symbols, arithmetical symbols, certain scientific symbols are added, we find that there are not so many symbols after all. The Fortran programming language, as an example, which is a widely used language, has only 47 characters: the 26 alphabetic characters (upper case only), the ten digit symbols, and only eleven special characters (see figure 2.9). To code these into unique patterns of binary digits, all that is required is a group of six binary digits to represent each of the 47 characters with some spare.

A group of two binary digits can represent *four* unique patterns; 00, 01, 10, 11. A group of three binary patterns can be used to represent *eight* unique patterns; a group of four can provide *sixteen*. Have you noticed anything so

FORTRAN	BASIC
A B C D E F G H I J K L M N O P Q R S T U V W X Y Z 0 1 2 3 4 5 6 7 8 9 ( ) * + - / £ , = . "space"	A B C D E F G H I J K L M N O P Q R S T U V W X Y Z 0 1 2 3 4 5 6 7 8 9 ( ) * + - / £ , = . "space" ; > < ↑ ↓ " :

Figure 2.9 These are the only characters which a programmer can use when writing in Fortran or Basic. Note that only capital letters are used.

Figure 2.10 Each two-state component can hold either binary 0 or binary 1 at any given instant. All possible combinations for 1 to 6 components are shown.

far? Two bits give 4, three bits 8, four bits 16, i.e. one more bit *doubles the previous number* of unique patterns. Thus, five bits should give 16 × 2, i.e. 32 patterns (and this can be seen to be true in figure 2.10), and six bits give 64.

A group of five bits would be too small to contain the 47 characters of the Fortran programming language, but a group of six bits is sufficient with 19 spare.

Figure 2.11 shows one method of representing our everyday characters into unique patterns of bits. Thus,

100001 = A   100010 = B   etc.

A group of six bits is a common grouping to represent up to 64 characters but some coding methods employ more characters making use of an eight-bit grouping to provide 256 unique patterns. In computer terminology, the grouping of six or eight bits is called a **byte** (seven is left out deliberately). One byte can hold one character, but two or more bytes are frequently combined together to form one memory word. The Control Data Corporation CDC 6500 computer, for example, has a byte of six bits, but a word length of 60 bits. Therefore, ten characters may be contained in one word, or, if a number has to be contained (as a binary number, of course), then one number equivalent to fifteen decimal digits when printed out can be contained in one word. This is quite an enormous number but then CDC computers are used in mathematical and scientific applications. Most current microcomputers have only eight bits as their word length and have to combine several bytes together when using large numbers.

The computers we have been discussing so far are those which contain their information internally as a series of binary digits. This type of computer is called a **digital computer** because the information is presented as individual or separate (discrete) units – the individual

1 bit	2 bits	3 bits	4 bits	5 bits	6 bits
0	00	000	0000	00000	000000
1	01	001	0001	00001	000001
	10	010	0010	00010	000010
	11	011	0011	00011	000011
		100	0100	00100	000100
		101	0101	00101	000101
		110	0110	00110	000110
		111	0111	00111	000111
			1000	01000	001000
			1001	01001	001001
			1010	01010	001010
			1011	01011	001011
			1100	01100	001100
			1101	01101	001101
			1110	01110	001110
			1111	01111	001111
				10000	010000
				10001	010001
				10010	010010
				10011	010011
				10100	010100
				10101	010101
				10110	010110
				10111	010111
				11000	011000
				11001	011001
				11010	011010
				11011	011011
				11100	011100
				11101	011101
				11110	011110
				11111	011111
					100000
					100001
					100010
					100011
					100100
					100101
					100110
					100111
					101000
					101001
					101010
					101011
					101100
					101101
					101110
					101111
					110000
					110001
					110010
					110011
					110100
					110101
					110110
					110111
					111000
					111001
					111010
					111011
					111100
					111101
					111110
					111111

Character Description	Printed Symbol	Internal machine 6-bit pattern	Character Description	Printed Symbol	Internal machine 6-bit pattern
Zero	0	00 0000	At	@	10 0000
One	1	00 0001		A	10 0001
Two	2	00 0010		B	10 0010
Three	3	00 0011		C	10 0011
Four	4	00 0100		D	10 0100
Five	5	00 0101		E	10 0101
Six	6	00 0110		F	10 0110
Seven	7	00 0111		G	10 0111
Eight	8	00 1000		H	10 1000
Nine	9	00 1001		I	10 1001
Colon	:	00 1010		J	10 1010
Semi-colon	;	00 1011		K	10 1011
Less than	<	00 1100		L	10 1100
Equals	=	00 1101		M	10 1101
Greater than	>	00 1110		N	10 1110
Question mark	?	00 1111		O	10 1111
Space		01 0000		P	11 0000
Exclamation	!	01 0001		Q	11 0001
Quotes	"	01 0010		R	11 0010
Hash mark	#	01 0011		S	11 0011
Pound	£	01 0100		T	11 0100
Percentage	%	01 0101		U	11 0101
Ampersand	&	01 0110		V	11 0110
Apostrophe	'	01 0111		W	11 0111
Left Parenthesis	(	01 1000		X	11 1000
Right Parenthesis	)	01 1001		Y	11 1001
Asterisk	*	01 1010		Z	11 1010
Plus	+	01 1011	L.H. Bracket	[	11 1011
Comma	,	01 1100	Dollar	$	11 1100
Hyphen/Minus	–	01 1101	R.H. Bracket	]	11 1101
Stop	.	01 1110		↑	11 1110
Solidus	/	01 1111		↓	11 1111

Figure 2.11 An example of a 64-character set, using 6 bits to determine each character.

binary zero or binary one. Another class exists, which shall not be discussed in any detail, called **analogue** computers. This type has its information in the form of *physical* information (as in Physics), e.g. a temperature reading or a pressure reading. Here the information is of a continuous nature, although it may vary, but it can be sensed at pre-determined intervals, in the way that a nurse can take the temperature of a patient at any given time via a thermometer and react accordingly.

What computers do

Having looked at the basic components which comprise a computer, we must now be clear about one feature. Essentially, a computer is capable of performing only *four* basic operations. After a few moments of studying figure 2.6, these become obvious. Clearly, input and ouput operations have to be performed in order to place information from the outside world into the internal world of the CPU, and vice versa. With the existence of an arithmetic unit, obviously computers must be capable of performing the four fundamental arithmetical operations. In the processing of data, we saw that data has to move around in the CPU and, furthermore, programmers have the means of organising related data items into lists within main memory. Finally, computers are very good at comparison and logical operations.

Although not mentioned before, the arithmetic unit has circuitry which not only performs arithmetic but also logical operations (the AND, OR, NOT, etc, operations). Consequently, the full name is the **arithmetic and logic unit** (ALU). Comparison operations in computers take the form of comparing two numbers (or letters) and finding out which is the larger (or further down the alphabet), the smaller, or whether they are equal. This can be explained by reference to a traffic intersection under computer-controlled traffic lights. If a build-up of cars on the main intersection is greater than, let us say, 20, then the timing of the lights can be changed to favour the main road traffic. Here a computer would compare at pre-set intervals the number of cars and compare it with 20. Whilst the build-up is less than 20, the timing is not altered, but when the number is equal to or greater than 20, then the timing pattern is changed.

No matter how much a computer costs, be it £50 or £5 million, these are the only fundamental operations which it can perform. The more expensive machines work at higher speeds and will have much larger memories (i.e. many more locations), but they will still be capable of performing only:

Input and output operations
Arithmetic operations
Comparison and logical operations
Movement of data.

It follows that computer programming languages can contain only instructions which relate to the above four. That is why the Fortran programming language, one of the earliest and still widely used, has a standard vocabulary of a mere seventeen words.

Yet, what about all the wonderful things which computers are capable of doing – landing men on the moon, controlling the traffic flow in some of the worlds major cities, playing and winning chess at tournament level, helping to diagnose illnesses? The extraordinary thing is that all these tasks and many more are carried out by a computer using only these four fundamental operations. The skill (some prefer to call it a craft or even an art) of a programmer lies in his or her ability to break down a task into an interplay between these four basic functions.

Why computers are so useful

However, we have not discussed these operations with a mind to examining the art of programming but rather with the intention of demonstrating why computers are of such value to mankind, in other words of discussing those characteristics which make computers useful machines.

In December 1979, Stan Barrett was the first person to break the sound barrier on land and to drive at 739.666 miles per hour. This is equivalent to 1085 feet per second. But the speeds with which electrical signals pass within the CPU are almost a million times faster, approximately that of light, namely 186 000 miles per second.

It is this speed which enables the computer to perform many thousands (even millions in the larger machines) of calculations per second. One large mainframe computer, the CDC 6500, can transfer internally ten million items of data within one second. Such speeds are beyond our comprehension, rather like our inability to comprehend the vast reaches of space and time. In order to quantify internal computer speeds we have to talk in terms of microseconds (millionths of a second) or even in nanoseconds (thousand-millionths of a second).

When we remember that, in the main, computers are involved in arithmetic, comparison, logical and movement of data operations, then this speed factor is crucial to an appreciation of their value. It is this speed which brings tomorrow's weather forecast today, enables seats to be booked on aircraft, and permits the cutting of red-hot steel into various sizes as it rolls along a running board. One oft-quoted example is the manual indexing of the complete works of St. Thomas Aquinas (involving approximately 13 million words). It would have taken fifty scholars forty years to accomplish, whereas, with the aid of a computer, this feat was achieved by a few scholars in less than one year. Computers then by their speed allow us to possess tomorrow's knowledge today and within our own lifetimes.

A second important ability is that computers can store vast amounts of information which can be sifted through and relevant details presented within seconds. More and more details are being amassed and not just by administrative departments. Science alone generates over six million new facts each year. It has become more expensive to house the information than the people generating it. Currently, microfilm is being used where possible to reduce the volume of paper. But this is a temporary solution. The advantage of computers is that they can store vast amounts of information in an extremely compact form. To cope with the future, microtechnology is going to have to be used more and more, and not only will the information be stored but it will be found and displayed for us at the touch of a few buttons or even by calling it up verbally.

As a third characteristic, computers, unlike frail human beings, do not become bored or tired and lose concentration when performing highly repetitive work. If a computer has to compute a million numbers, it will calculate the first and the last with equal diligence. This enables us to trust the results generated by computers and to place a confidence in their ability which we cannot always place in humans.

Of course, the mass media enjoys highlighting any "mistakes" produced by computers, such as the repeated demands for "£0.0 to be settled within thirty days, otherwise court proceedings, ..." However, the computer is only

capable of doing what it is told to do. If the human beings who design a given application make a mistake, in invoicing customers for example, then it is hardly fair to lay the blame on the computer. When correctly programmed, computers are far more accurate than human beings.

So these characteristics of speed, storage and retrieval ability, diligence and accuracy are the virtues of the traditional computer which have led us to depend upon them. In the next chapter, we shall look at the microcomputer and see where it fits in relation to the traditional computer and see how it will revolutionise our world as we know it today.

There is just one more point which needs to be made for a full appreciation of the computer. Many dictionaries tend to emphasise the calculative nature of computers. We may be forgiven if this is the image that we hold, especially when we recall that the binary number system is used to represent information held in store, that its main operations consist of arithmetic operations and comparing numbers, and that the early computers were designed specifically as calculating devices.

However, we must not confuse a method of coding information and the basic operations of a computer with its primary ability of handling information. A computer is admirably suited to handle any information and first and foremost it is an *information processor*. That is, it can receive information, perform some basic operations on that information, and produce results according to a pre-determined program. As it becomes increasingly difficult for human minds to cope and sort through information, the more relevant it becomes to call in the computer. One perfect example of this is in the general practitioner's surgery.

Currently, information is "stored" on each patient in a small envelope about five by eight inches. The outside contains areas where the patient's name and address may be recorded, the patient's National Health number, occupation, doctor's name, together with the County area stamp. Inside is a form which enables the doctor to record the date of a visit, with a line so that the nature of the patient's present complaint and treatment can be noted. All relevant details of a patient's history must be contained in the envelope together with letters from hospitals, etc. As we all know, GPs are busy people. A surgery may last about two-and-a-half hours and many patients will arrive during this time. The BMA (British Medical Association) has allocated about ten minutes of surgery time per patient. As each patient enters for his or her consultation, the envelope must be readily available so that any treatment by the doctor (or locum) may be related to any previous treatment.

A friend of mine who acts as a locum has commented upon the hazards of this primitive storage system. A patient enters, and if the details in the envelope are numerous, he could spend more than the ten minutes merely reading them. The cards are not necessarily in chronological order, nor the letters from hospital consultants. It is quite often a jumble. We may think that the doctor can recall all our details from his mind, but a typical patient ratio is two and a half thousand patients per doctor. Previous treatments are recorded in handwriting and thus liable to be indecipherable; in some cases previous treatments are simply not recorded because the GP does not have the time to meticulously record all details on every patient. This archaic system is so ripe for computerisation, for the benefit of GPs as much as patients, that it must come.

Were records on a computer system, then the GP would only have to request each record and within seconds be presented with all relevant details relating to that patient. All previous illnesses would be listed, aversion to any particular drug, current drugs and dosage, together with important facts such as a lessening of one type of drug dosage to avoid poisoning, details of hospital notes, dates for follow-up treatments, and so on – facts which the GP cannot be expected to carry at the forefront of his mind for two thousand or so patients. In a computerised system, the GP, at the touch of a few terminal keys, could have access to all that he needs to know instead of pulling out a jumble of details. The traditional computer could help but would not be cost-effective. Microcomputers, on the other hand, are cost-effective. This is what we shall consider in the next chapter.

Three
The Microprocessor and the Microcomputer

In 1950, the National United States Census was made possible by ENIAC, a computer costing then $500 000. Today the same computing power can be ordered by mail for less than $10. This has been made possible by advances in microelectronic technology which have led to the development of the microprocessor. But what exactly is a microprocessor? We can best illustrate this by drawing upon a few concepts raised in the previous chapter.

The traditional computer (figure 3.1), that is the central processing unit comprising the arithmetic/logic unit, control unit and store, is often divided into two main parts. The first consists of both the control unit and the arithmetic/logic unit and is referred to collectively as the **central processor** (CP). The second part is the store itself. The **microprocessor** is no different to the central processor of a traditional computer except that the traditional central processor is larger and more expensive than the smaller and cheaper microprocessor, and has been around since the 1940s whereas the microprocessor has been available since 1971.

By itself the microprocessor is not a fully fledged computer. In the same way that the traditional CP requires a store, input and output devices, auxiliary storage devices, as well as a set of operating system programs to turn the hardware into a functioning computer, so the microprocessor requires these components in order to become a **microcomputer.** Figure 3.2 shows such a system.

Essentially, there is no difference between a traditional computer and a microcomputer; both require the same basic components, both function in the same way. A computer program written for a traditional computer could well be used without amendment on a microcomputer. The difference between the two is a matter of size and cost. These two variants can affect the performance of the microcomputer resulting in advantages as well as disadvantages. But before discussing these in any detail, let us first look at what is meant by the smallness of microprocessors and see how this has affected their cost.

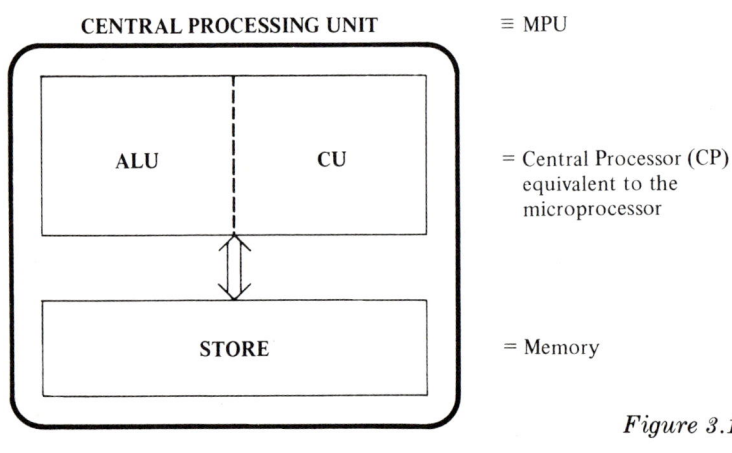

Figure 3.1

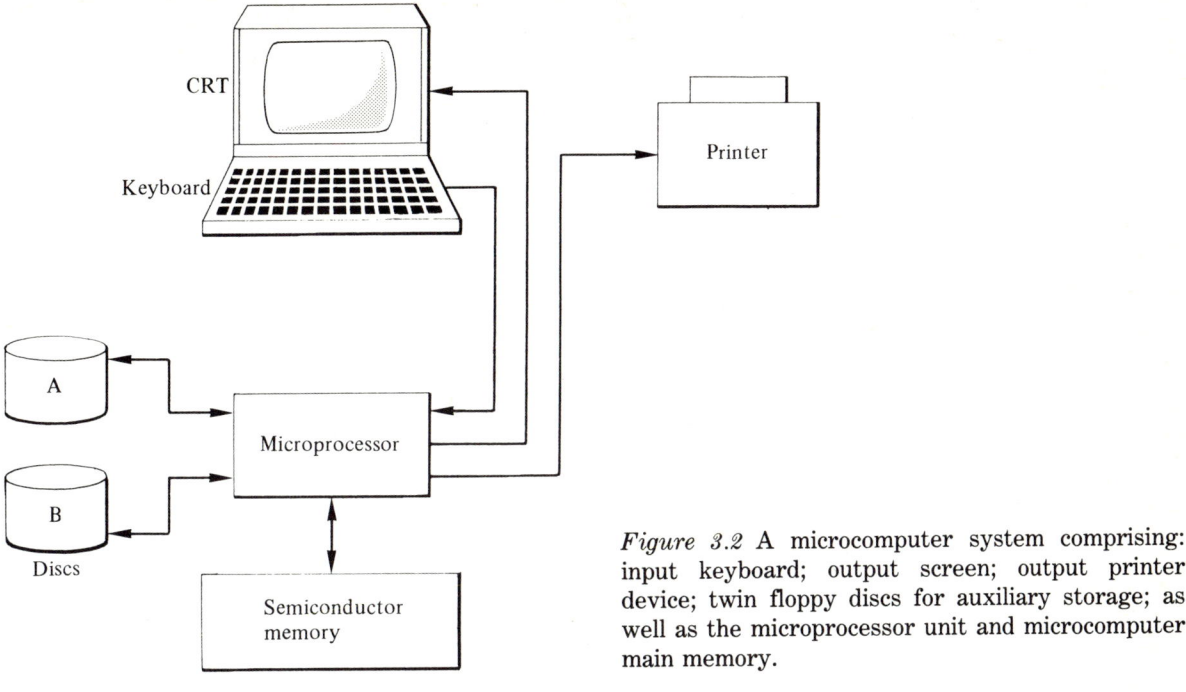

Figure 3.2 A microcomputer system comprising: input keyboard; output screen; output printer device; twin floppy discs for auxiliary storage; as well as the microprocessor unit and microcomputer main memory.

The technology generations

During the thirty-five years or so since computers first began to appear, the basic technology for their construction has undergone considerable changes. In the early days of the 1940s, their performance was limited by the available electronic technology, namely vacuum tubes. These were relatively large as anyone who remembers the old wireless sets can testify. The tubes generated a great deal of heat which resulted in their having a short operating life as will as the need for air conditioning. ENIAC, the first all-electronic computer, developed at Pennsylvania University in America had 18 000 tubes. (However, since the Official Secrets Act applying to British activities during the Second World War is gradually being lifted, it is hinted that England in fact developed the first electronic computer.) Larger machines with even more tubes were impractical since more time would have been spent in finding and replacing defective tubes than in the actual running of the computer. It has become customary to talk of this early era as the first generation of computers.

Although the transistor was developed in 1947, it was not used generally in computers until 1952. It seems strange to record that computer designers did not seem to appreciate for some years how necessary this much smaller component was for the very survival of the infant computer. Without the transistor, the computer would have met with a premature end.

The second generation of computers, then, made use of the transistor. The advantage gained by this technology was a smaller and more reliable component which consumed less power and generated less heat than vacuum tubes. This enabled more circuits to be used in computers leading to larger machines (i.e. in circuit complexity, not size), capable of being applied to more complex applications than the first generation.

GENERA-TION	ELECTRONIC COMPONENT	ADVANTAGES	DISADVANTAGES	COMMENTS
1st generation 1940–52	Vacuum tubes	Vacuum tubes were the only electronic components available	Large-size Generated heat Air-conditioning required Unreliable Constant maintenance	Manual assembly of individual components into a functioning unit
2nd generation 1952–64	Transistors	Smaller-size Less heat generated More reliable Faster	Air-conditioning required Maintenance	As above
3rd generation 1964–71	Integrated circuits	Even smaller size Even lower heat generation Less power required Even more reliable Faster still	Initially, problems with manufacture	Less human labour at assembly stage
4th generation 1971–	Large-scale integrated circuits	No air-conditioning Minimal maintenance High component density Cheapest	Currently (1981), less powerful than mainframe computers	As above

Figure 3.3 Generation chart of electronic components.

In both generations, however, the basic component was a discrete or separate entity which had to be assembled by hand into functioning circuits. It was the cost of labour at this assembly stage that became increasingly expensive. In one of the early machines, the Harvard Mark I, an electro-mechanical computer, some 500 miles of wire were required to link the various components together – all by hand!

The breakthrough which eventually led to microelectronics came just a few years after the invention of the transistor but it took almost a decade before the techniques of manufacturing this new technology were mastered. Once this happened, it became possible to combine a handful of circuits into an integrated whole on a small surface less than 5 mm ($\frac{1}{4}$ inch) square. This new technology was called **integrated circuits** (ICs) and its real impact was in elimi-

nating the labour costs previously required. It was in 1964 (approximately) that integrated circuits began to be used in any number in the construction of computers, thereby ushering in the third generation. At first, only a handful, about ten, components could be combined. This became known as small-scale integration (SSI). As the techniques for manufacturing ICs improved, it became possible to combine up to a hundred—medium-scale integration (MSI). Today, it is possible to pack 20 000 components onto the same small area of 5 mm square by 1 mm thick—large-scale integration (LSI). By 1985, it is expected that this volume will increase to a million (very large-scale integration, VLSI). (See diagram of generations, figure 3.3 and figure 3.4.)

Although it was in the early 1950s that computer engineers began to realise the excit-

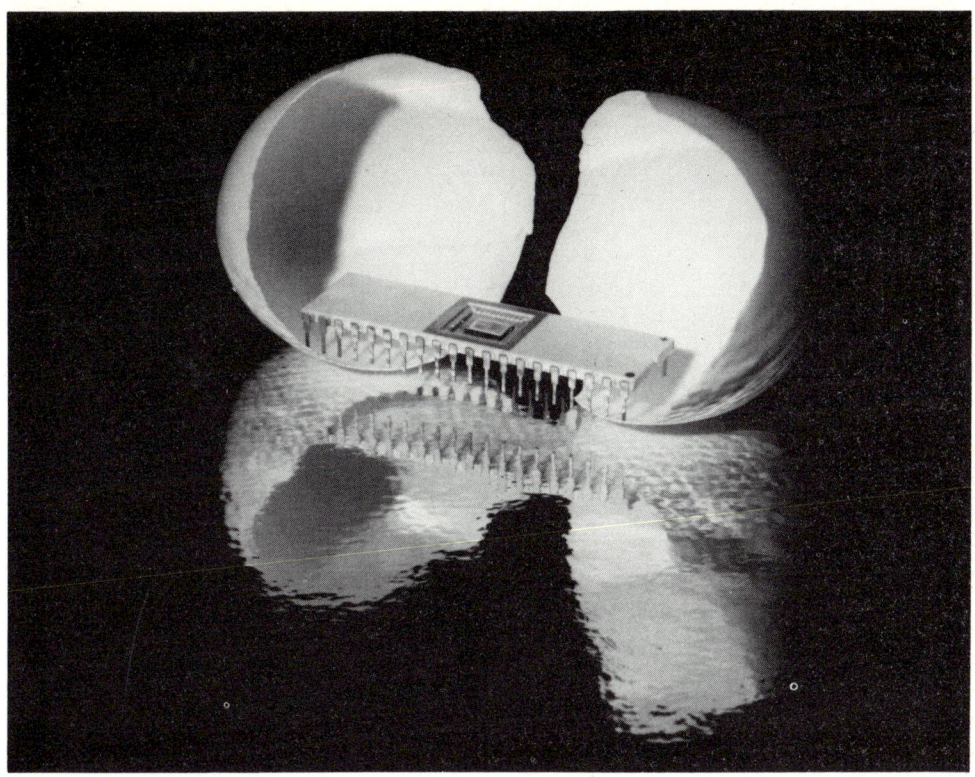

Figure 3.4 The tiny chip some 5 mm square by 1 mm thick contains many thousands of electronic circuits. It is housed on a plastic base of about 40 mm long. The chip "interfaces" with the outside world via fine wires leading to the metal connections coming out of the plastic base.
(*Courtesy: Intel Corporation*)

ing possibilities of ICs, several key requirements in their manufacturing process had to be developed. The fabrication process of combining so many electronic circuits on such a small area is discussed in chapter 5. For the present, we must assume that it is technically possible to produce computers equivalent to the power of ENIAC (indeed, larger) with its 18 000 vacuum tubes, on a small area of silicon, making it feasible to mass-produce "ENIACs" so that their individual cost drops from $500 000 (1950) to $10 (1980).

In order to appreciate this point, it is necessary to recall from chapter 2 that computers of any size or cost are only capable of performing a limited number of basic operations. This might appear to be a limitation but in practice becomes their very strength. What we are saying is that the CP of a traditional computer can be mass-produced at a very low cost partly because the labour costs of joining separate components can be eliminated and substituted by a process involving chemical and photographical means.

But this is not all. As we have seen, a CP requires a memory in order to become a functional computer. It happens that microelectronic technology can mass-produce such memories in the same way that microprocessors are mass produced.

Microcomputer memories

The main memories of a microcomputer are as cheap and as small as the microprocessor itself. When combined, the two units form a central processing unit of comparable ability to the CPU of many traditional computers and are called a microprocessor unit (MPU). (See figure 3.1)

Computing abounds with jargon terms which form a very effective barrier for keeping laymen at bay. However, although a curse to the layman, to professionals in a particular field – medicine, law, publishing, jobbing, accountancy, science, etc. – it is a shorthand method for communicating with each other. So why not have jargon in computing? This next section contains several jargon terms which if mastered will enable you to compete with the most jargon-orientated salesman.

The memory unit of the microcomputer is often referred to as a **random access memory** or RAM because, like the main memory of the traditional computer, information can be placed into this memory by input devices and information can be taken out and written in human-readable format by output devices.

RAM memories, because they enable information to be "read out" from them and "written into" them, are more properly called Read/Write memories. The information can be stored for a given period of time or can be changed according to the requirements of an application program. When a microcomputer is switched off, the information in RAM is lost and can no longer be used.

Another class of memory exists in a microcomputer which will not allow its contents to be lost and which will remain intact even when the computer is switched off so that it can be readily available for a future occasion. Typically, the type of information which this memory contains is a program. The memory is called a **read only memory** or ROM because the information it contains can only be used or "read", not just once, however, but any number of times. A copy only of the ROM program may be obtained. This is not so strange as it may appear.

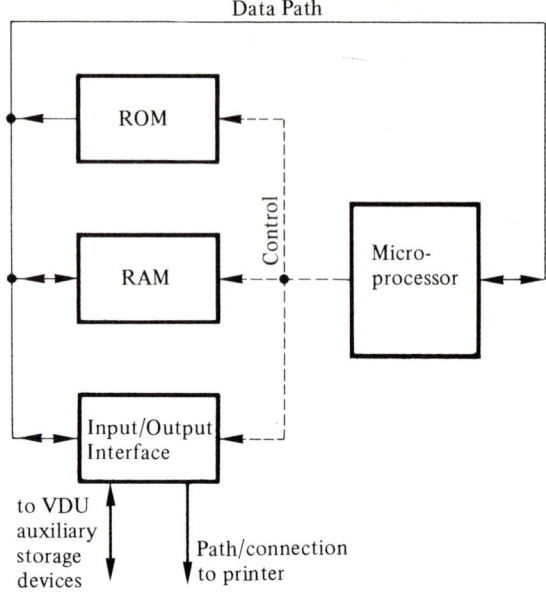

Figure 3.5 A microcomputer comprising the microprocessor (ALU and CU), the ROM and RAM memories together with an input/output interface board connecting the microcomputer to external devices.

The dotted lines show the *control* paths leading from the microprocessor to the other parts (modules) of the system.

The other lines show the data paths permitting information to pass between individual modules.

Let us take an example. A pocket calculator is designed so that, when two numbers are entered with, for example, a plus symbol, the addition function will be performed. A "program" exists which is able to detect the addition symbol as distinct from a multiplication or percentage symbol and will ensure that addition is carried out. The program needs to be stored in ROM so that the user cannot destroy or interfere with its contents and thereby render the calculator useless. Similarly for programs which control the operation of a washing machine, electric oven or petrol pump.

The development of programs for computers, especially the operating system software which drives the hardware of the machine, is a particularly expensive procedure. It is not unusual for many hundreds of thousands of pounds to be spent in the development of an operating system destined for a machine priced £100 or more. Such software becomes cost-effective when the development costs can be spread over many buyers, each one buying a copy of the original. Obviously, it is sensible to protect this software by placing it in a ROM so that every time the machine is switched on it is readily available for use but not for interference.

RAM and ROM memories are the two main types of memory used in microcomputers. Being manufactured on silicon chips, they too are cheap when mass-produced. With the ROM memory, since it is impossible to alter the information once it has been "fixed" into the chip, it is necessary to ensure that the information which it will contain is absolutely correct, otherwise the chip will be useless.

A variation of the ROM chip called a **programmable read only memory** or PROM also can only have its contents "read out". Where it differs from the ROM is that, by using a special device known as a prom-programmer, informa-

tion can be recorded on the chip. This can be an arduous task and is best performed by a specialist rather than the general microcomputer user. The advantage for the specialist is that he can place his own binary information or program into the chip after the chip has been made. Once the chip has been programmed, however, its contents cannot be changed or altered since the fusible links are set permanently by the prom-programmer.

Another type of memory chip *can* have its binary contents changed. This is the EPROM chip, the E standing for erasable. When the chip is exposed to ultraviolet light all the binary information is reset to a state of binary 1 by a process of ionisation, thereby destroying the original information. This type of memory chip is more expensive than the PROM chip. Special prom-programmer units can be used to re-program the chip. Typical writing speeds of these devices are 512 characters per minute. Once re-programmed, the EPROM chip is used in read-only mode.

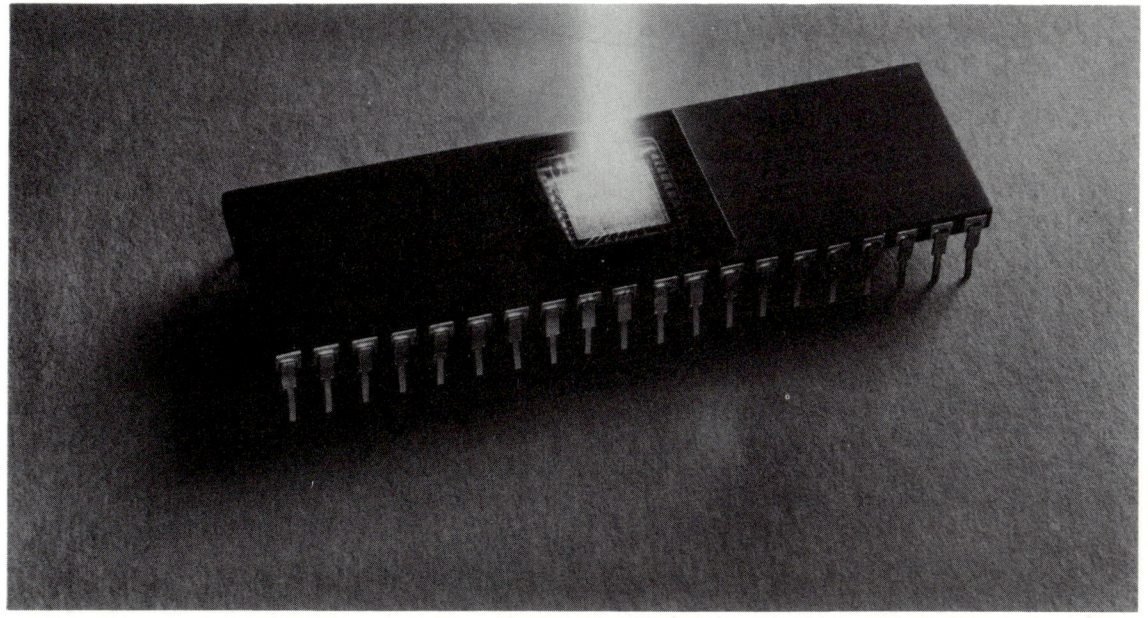

Figure 3.6 A single-chip computer comprising all the units as shown in figure 3.5. It contains an EPROM memory rather than a ROM memory which can be erased when a beam of ultraviolet light passes through the transparent window. The device may then be re-programmed for use in some other product. (*Courtesy: Intel Corporation*)

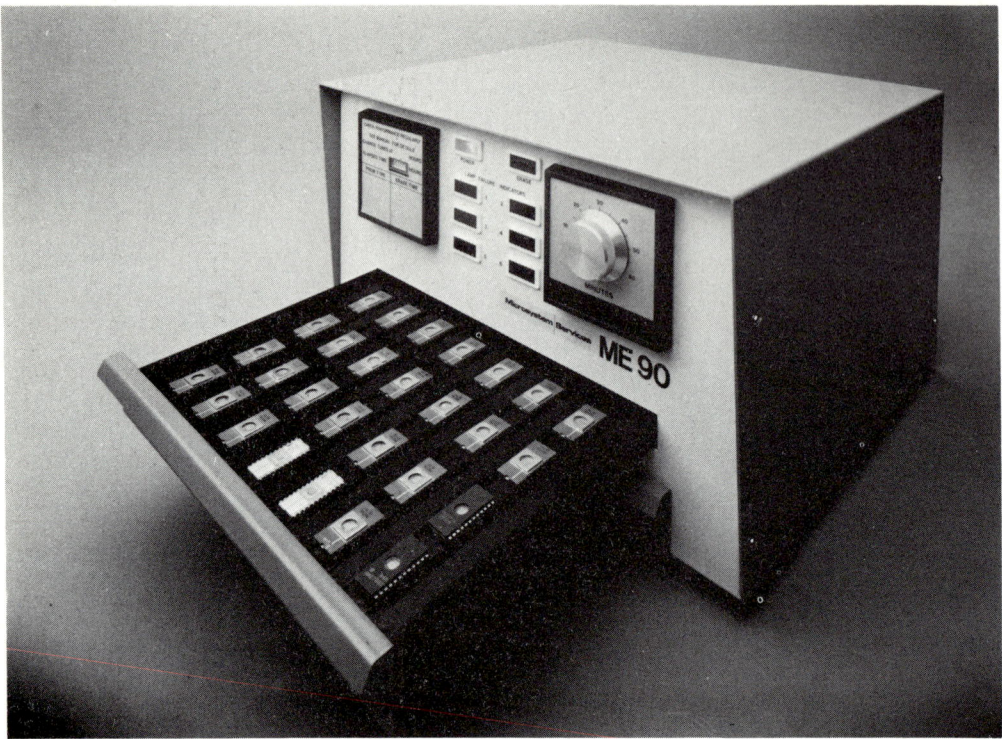

Figure 3.7 An EPROM programmer device.
(*Courtesy: Microsystem Services Ltd*)

There is also the electrically alterable ROM chip or EAROM. Binary information of either 1s or 0s can be directly entered into the chip. The EPROM and the EAROM are similar in one way, therefore, namely that each can have new information written into the chip so that they can be used time and again in different program applications. There are differences too. In the case of the EAROM, information tends to fade after it has been read out from the chip a certain number of times, whereas the EPROM chip can have its information read out any number of times without this happening. After 10^9 reads (1 000 000 000), information must be written back into the EAROM chip. This process is known as 10^9 *reads before write*.

Although this number of reads may seem enormous, one program could well access the information stored in an EAROM chip many thousands of times in the course of one execution of that program. It would not take too

many similar runs to exhaust the number of reads allowed. Consequently, the applications for EAROM chips is limited, typically to situations where tables of information are read into the RAM memory of the microcomputer once during the execution of a program, and all subsequent use of those tables is made from RAM rather than from the EAROM chip.

A second and far less important difference between the two chips is that the EPROM can alter states from binary 1 to binary 0 only (all states being set to 1s initially by exposure to ultraviolet light), whereas the EAROM chip can have a binary 1 changed to binary 0 and vice versa.

Future memories

The search for cheaper and higher capacity chips is a current obsession in the computer industry and no wonder since the rewards are

Figure 3.8 This magnetic bubble memory (MBM) from Intel is a high-density one megabit (1 048 576 bits) memory. Information held in this memory is not lost when the power supply is switched off. (*Courtesy: Intel Corporation*)

large. Certain developments in **magnetic bubble memories** (MBMs) hold a promising future at the time of writing. Bubble memories retain their information even when the power is switched off (called non-volatile memories). These chips are capable of storing one million bits of binary information and future developments will increase this capacity even further to 10 million bits before 1985. They will pose a threat to moving magnetic devices such as magnetic tapes and discs currently used to hold large amounts of binary information. But bubble memories still have a long way to go before they can compete on a cost basis with these other magnetic devices.

The technology was first developed at Bell Laboratories, in 1967. The bubbles are magnetised *domains* in a thin film of material of an opposite polarity. The domains or bubbles are formed when a magnetic field is applied to the magnetised film. The presence or absence of a bubble denotes a binary digit, absence being binary 0, presence being binary 1. Another type of MBM developed by IBM has two different bubbles, each one representing either a binary one or a binary zero.

One magnetic bubble memory chip developed by Intel can hold 1 048 576 bits on a garnet wafer about 14 millimetres (0.6 inches) square. In combination, these chips could contain whole books and even a small library in a highly compact form. It will not be too long before we shall be able to carry such devices around in our pockets. What is more, these forms of memory may well displace the present auxiliary storage units which, in the case of the floppy disc drives, can form over 50% of the total hardware cost of a general microcomputer system.

A single chip microcomputer

Figure 3.9 relates the conventional diagram of the traditional CPU to the conventional diagram for a microprocessor unit. When the microprocessor together with RAM and ROM (or PROM/EPROM) memories are built onto one chip, we talk about a single chip computer. Having seen the relationship between the microcomputer and the traditional computer, and having discussed necessary technical details concerning both, we can now begin to consider the value of these micros to both industry and commercial organisations.

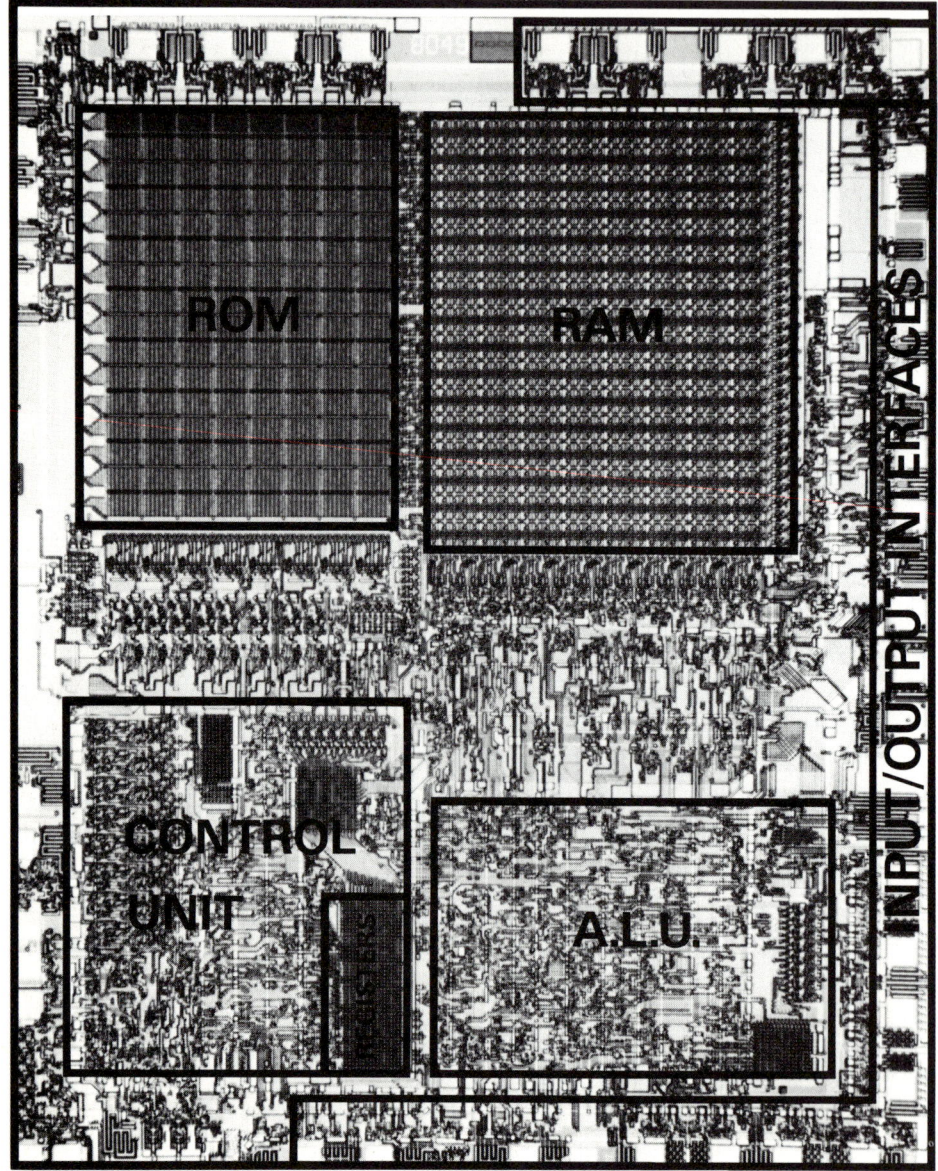

Figure 3.9 A tiny microcomputer contained on an area 5 mm square by 1 mm thick. It consists of all the essential units of a traditional computer. Note the fine wires leading from the chip edges to form connections to the outside world (see also Figure 4.1) (*Courtesy: Intel Corporation*)

Four
The Chips

A microcomputer consisting of a micro-processor and some memory chips can be integrated onto a single chip. This chip is of little use to people who require the services of a centralised computer centre in order to run their payroll, client/job costing, their mailing lists, etc. For such typical data processing activities, a much more elaborate and, therefore, more expensive microcomputer system is required.

On the other hand, the little chip bursting with computing power is ideal for many industrial processes involving some control currently performed by an electro-mechanical device. In order to be able to decide which type of microcomputer is suitable for a given application, it is necessary to be aware of the features of the different classes of microcomputers.

The chip level

At the chip level, all the functions of a CPU are contained on one small slice of silicon. The microprocessor has the ability to provide arithmetic and logic operations, and the control unit coordinates the activities of a program embedded in a memory chip. This program, designed to perform a specific application, is held in a ROM, PROM or EPROM chip. Via an input device, the ever-changing data for a given application is entered into RAM. The result(s) from the computer program is handled by an output device, which may turn off the electric oven, select the spin programme on the washing machine, set off an alarm, or, indeed, be displayed onto a small screen.

In this last situation, the display may be made by **light emitting diodes** (LEDs), by **liquid crystal displays** (LCDs), or by **fluorescent gas-discharge displays** (Digitrons). LEDs are small, solid-state devices which emit a light, usually red, when a current is passed through them. They are easy to manufacture and therefore cheap. The LCDs use a chemical in liquid form which changes its chemical structure when a voltage is applied. In order that the LCDs are seen, a light must fall upon them and, as a consequence, they cannot be used in poor light. The Digitrons require a fairly high voltage as well as additional circuitry which increases their cost above that of LEDs. However, these fluorescent displays are larger and clearer than LEDs and are usually green, although yellow and orange displays are also in use.

The advantages of microchip computers are a reduction in cost and size of components, increase in performance and reliability, and scope for innovation. Most industrial and process firms can now afford to purchase computing power even though changes in existing production methods may not prove to be so inexpensive, but what a firm cannot afford is to lose out to its competitors who will begin to employ microchips.

This microcomputer on a chip can cost anywhere between £5 and £50. To keep to this low cost per unit, they must be produced in high volume. For instance, a microprocessor chip to control the fuel injection for a motor car or the programme control for a washing machine will be used in their thousands.

However, software skills are required to produce the program which will make the chip function in the correct way; engineering skills are also needed to interface the basic chip to

Figure 4.1 The tiny microelectronic device is capable of replacing a much larger electro-mechanical device. Yet these chips are cheaper, more reliable, far smaller and capable of much more intelligence through a controlling program held in ROM. (*Courtesy: Texas Instruments*)

input and ouput devices. By placing a new program in the EPROM chip, or by exchanging the ROM or PROM chip by another one with a different program, then the microprocessor is happy to perform some other task.

The board-level computer

For many applications, a single-chip computer is too limiting. Individual chips, each one representing one of the basic components of a computer system, such as RAM and ROM, input/output interfacing logic, MPU, timing clock, etc., can be combined onto a single board, typically some nine inches by five inches. The one board may contain a dozen or several dozen chips depending on the number of ROM/RAM memory chips. At the present time each chip may contain between 1K and 8K bits of information. The individual chips are arranged on what is called a **printed circuit board** (pcb) and

interlinked to provide a working system under the control of the microprocessor chip.

Such a board system may cost several hundreds of pounds and like the single-chip computer will have to be programmed and interfaced with input and output devices in order to provide some particular service. This level frequently has a limited keyboard usually in octal or hexadecimal (variations of binary) rather than a full keyboard with letters of the alphabet, decimal numbers, etc. Output displays employing LEDs, LCDs, or Digitrons may be in binary, octal or hexadecimal. If all our everyday characters were to be displayed, then the output display would cost far more than the actual board computer itself.

These computers can cost between £200 and £500 but are often limited to teaching and training courses. Beginners, especially when using the E&L MMD board with its clearly laid-out and labelled chips, quickly learn about

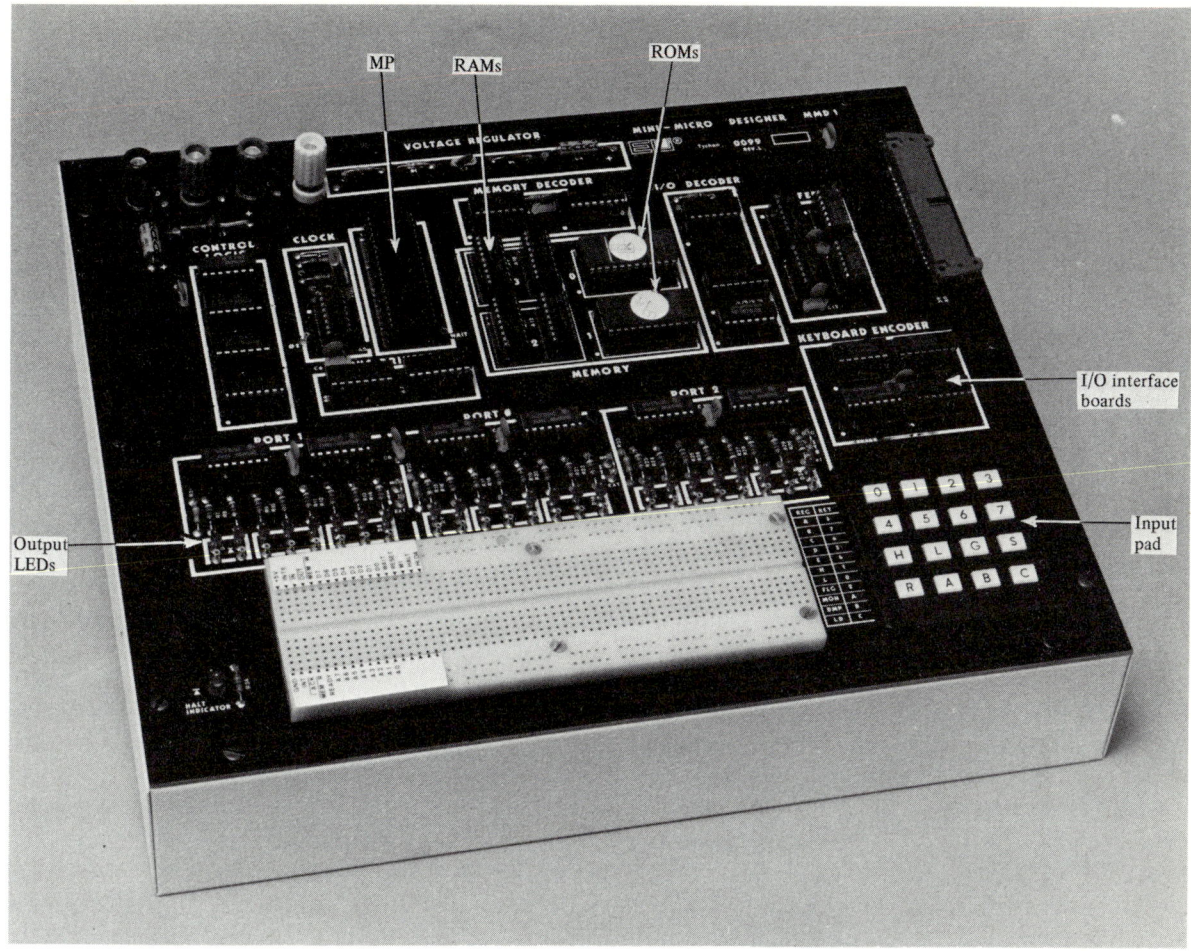

Figure 4.2 The board contains all the various chips which comprise a functioning microcomputer system. This particular model for use in training microelectronic engineers has 33 chips. Output is in the form of light emitting diodes (LEDs), usually red, which light up when a voltage is applied. When lit, the diode shows the presence of a binary one; when unlit, it "shows" the presence of a binary zero.
(Courtesy: E & L Instruments (UK) Ltd)

the fundamentals of microcomputers, the various types of chip, and the art of programming. However, the novice, in general, can quickly outgrow the single-board computer.

The multi-board microcomputer system

The single-chip computer costing anywhere between £5 and £50 depending on its complexity and degree of speciality is suited to process

control, instrumentation and communications. Many other applications require far greater computer facilities than those offered by the single-chip or board computer. In general, data-processing and commercial applications are such areas. Here, there is a need for much more sophisticated input/output devices than the limited entry buttons and display panel of the pocket calculator type. Figure 4.3 shows a VDU with QWERTY keyboard and a large

Figure 4.3 Typical multi-board microcomputer system comprising keyboard and VDU screen, for input and output, mini-floppy discs for auxiliary mass storage, and cabinet housing the microcomputer. (*Courtesy: Toshiba*)

mass storage facility provided by a floppy disc system.

Various boards, each containing some computer system function such as the input/output interfacing board, one or more ROM/RAM boards, a board with the MPU, the clock, etc., are all mounted on a single horizontal board known as the **mother board**. The individual boards are all interlinked through this mother board and usually housed together in one cabinet which, in effect, becomes the microcomputer itself. It may be of interest to mention that the actual cabinet itself may cost more than the technology which it houses. All peripheral devices have to be connected to the microcomputer cabinet to form a computer hardware system. Such a system will need additional system software to drive the hardware units, as well as application programs to perform specific data processing tasks such as client/job costing, word processing, invoicing, GPs patient records, etc.

Usually, the input/output device is a visual display unit where the keyboard acts as the input device and the cathode ray tube screen acts as the output display device. A printer will also be required for permanent copies if required. Storage for data, application programs, and for certain operating system software which cannot be held in ROM, is provided by some form of mass storage device. This may be a tape cassette system using ordinary music cassettes or a floppy disc storage system.

Vast amounts of information can be held on these devices. One floppy diskette can hold up to 250 000 characters on one side. If the disc is double-sided, like a record disc, then this figure can be doubled. When twin disc units are used, two diskettes can be available to the microcomputer system such that any one of the four surfaces can be accessed at any instant. Four sides provide one million characters or a **megabyte** (where each byte is equivalent to one character). Certain advances in mass storage devices allow twice the amount of information to be stored on a disc by packing the information closer together and therefore accessing two megabytes or two million characters of text at any instant. To give some idea, this book contains some 120 000 characters of text.

By removing one diskette and replacing it with another, a further one million characters

Figure 4.4 A typical cassette-based storage microcomputer system.
(*Courtesy: Research Machines*)

can be made available to the microcomputer. This process can go on indefinitely. Each diskette costs only £10 so that the amount of information which can be stored in a diskette system is relatively cheap and infinite. The driving units themselves, however, cost £1000 each.

Cassette versions are cheaper but much slower since the information they contain has to be accessed in a **serial** fashion, in the same way that a person requiring the fourth piece of music on a cassette tape has to "forward wind" over the first, second and third pieces until positioned at the start of the fourth. This is time consuming and can take several minutes since ordinary domestic tape recorders are used.

In the case of an LP record, the fourth piece of music can be accessed straight away by placing the needle over the fourth track (or band). This more direct access to information is the way a floppy disc system works, except that the system will position the reading/writing head ("needle") over the right information automatically and within a few thousandths of a second (milliseconds). Also, it will keep an account of where every program and item of data has been recorded, on which surface, and on which track of the diskette, and can display within a few milliseconds any information stored on any one of the four surfaces of either diskette in a twin disc-drive. It is this speed and ability to move to any track and any surface automatically that makes the disc system the only feasible existing mass storage device for data processing applications. Although possible with cassette tape systems, this device is extremely time consuming.

Figure 4.5 A diskette being removed from its envelope. An 8 inch (200 mm) standard diskette can hold up to 1 million characters.
(*Courtesy: IBM United Kingdom Ltd*)

Video discs

Cheaper mass storage devices are currently under development. To date, the floppy disc unit holds pride of place, but when it is realised that such a device accounts for almost half of the total cost of a complete microcomputer system, it makes sense to search out yet cheaper means. One of these is the video disc. At the moment, video discs are associated with the home entertainment market and are not suitable for use with mass storage of information in microcomputer systems.

However, new systems of video discs are beginning to emerge which could make the electronic office a reality within the next few years. The domestic video disc is used for TV or music. But the electronic office will use this device in a different way and should be called something else to avoid confusion. The current popular term is a "digital read after write device" or DRAW. Where it differs from floppy discs is that the device will be cheaper and capable of storing not only computer data but also virtually all forms of information such as text, still half-tone pictures, graphics, and voice. Current devices are already capable of storing one thousand million characters of information or one hundred thousand A4 pages.

An important aspect of video discs is their ability to produce information on a random basis. Unlike tapes which have only sequential

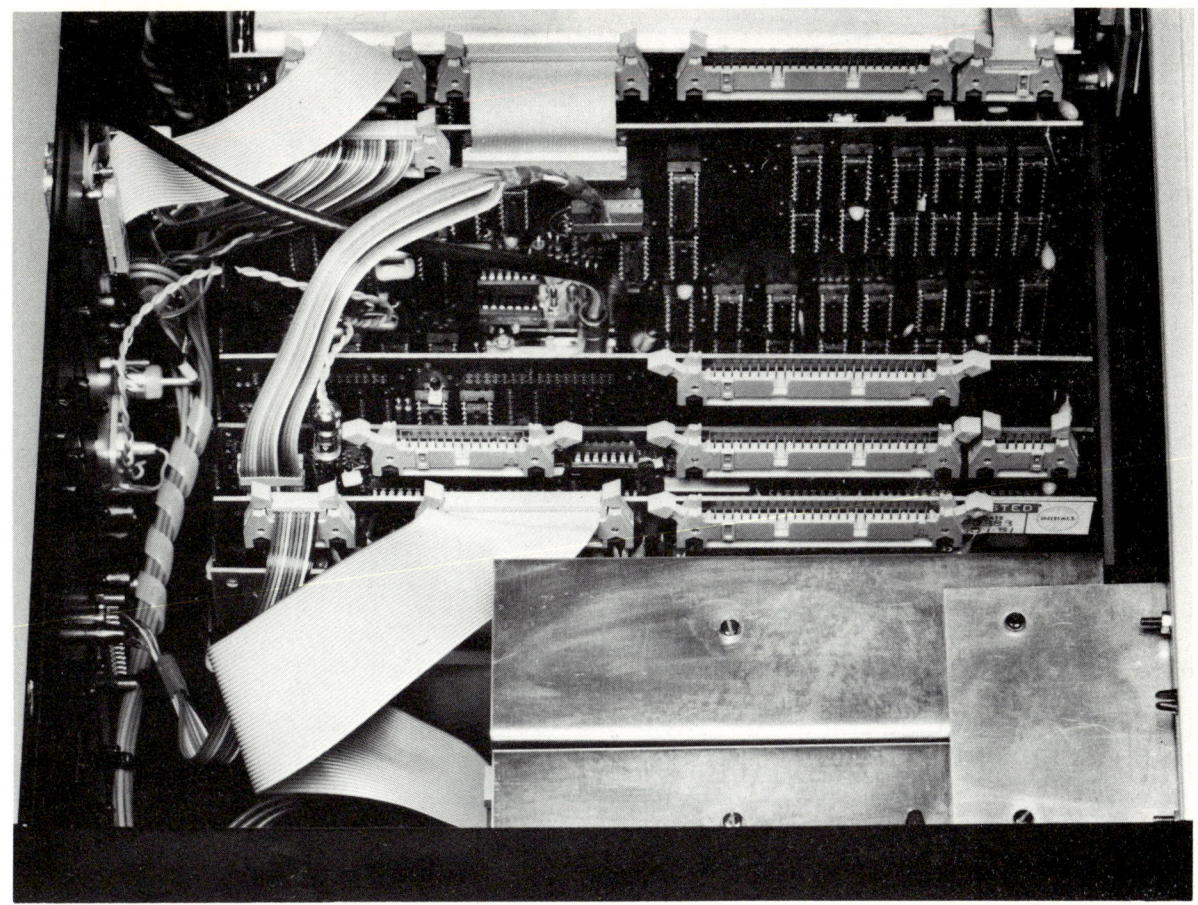

Figure 4.6 Inside a multi-board RM 380Z microcomputer cabinet. One board contains the microprocessor, another the ROM chips, one or more boards the RAM memory chips, other boards contain the I/O interfacing logic, timing control and such additional facilities as graphics. (Each board is shown as slotted in vertically.) (*Courtesy: Research Machines*)

output of information, that is the output is produced in the order in which it is input, rather like a film strip, these random devices will be capable of accessing any sequence of frames in any order. Information held in one area can be produced and "mixed in" with any information held elsewhere. An example of such versatility is shown in chapter 7 in relation to computer assisted learning for secondary schools. Current domestic players have a capacity of 54 000 frames, where each frame could represent one ordinary TV picture frame, permitting something like 30 minutes viewing time in one complete sequence per side.

ROMs, RAMs, EPROMs, EAROMs,

MBMs, floppy diskettes, and DRAW discs — each offer some individual feature not found in the others. Future systems will almost certainly see an integrating of different types of memory into a memory system tailored for a given application.

What is cheap?

We are now in a position to appreciate just what is cheap in a microcomputer system. To do this we need to look at the various component costs of the traditional computer. Seven components can be identified:

Figure 4.7 A ROM module board. Up to 21 chips may be contained on this single board (12 are shown in the photograph), each holding 1024 binary digits. (*Courtesy: Toshiba*)

The CPU comprising the CP and the memory
Input devices
Output devices
Mass storage auxiliary devices
Operating system software
Room space and air conditioning
Manpower – operators, maintenance engineers and systems programmers.

In the case of the microcomputer, it is the MPU which is cheap. This has been reduced by a factor of 100 so that a £50 000 minicomputer of yesterday can cost today a mere £500 when realised as a microcomputer. Although it is true that microelectronics are used in input and output devices, their cost has not been reduced by that much. A typical input and output device is the visual display unit, costing at least £500. If permanent copies are required, some form of printer must be purchased. Current prices lie between £500 and £2500. Disc drives for mass storage of data and programs cost £1000 and a twin disc system is necessary for most data processing applications. In order to drive all these peripheral units, operating system software is required. Now the basic cost of the microcomputer rises from the original £500 to anywhere up to £5000. Although such systems take up very little room and require no air conditioning, some form of maintenance, particularly for the peripheral units, will have to be considered. Finally, there is a question of reliable application programs. Some of these may well cost up to £5000 and even more, whether they be purchased from a software manufacturer or developed on-site.

The microcomputer power is cheap but the cost of the rest of the system has not altered that much. The enthusiasm of microprocessor manufacturers and computer scientists, as well as the interest of the mass media in anything to do with microelectronics, often overplay the "cheapness" factor of microcomputers. Frequently, the layperson is surprised and confused when eventually faced with realistic costs for a total system. However, despite these comments the fact is that the equivalent computing power of a machine cosing £50 000 between 1960 and 1970 can be bought today for £500. Even with additional units the total price is still within the means of most small companies, schools, even the home enthusiast. This is reflected in the slogan coined by Texas Instruments: "We have brought computing power to everyone."

What of future chip systems?

ENIAC had 18 000 valves; today a similar number of components can be packed onto a chip 5 mm square. But with the advent of very-large-scale integration (VLSI), a million components can be packed onto the same single chip, and, by 1985, reports indicate that it will be technically possible to have 10 million. What does this mean?

The world's largest computer, the CRAY, an enormous machine in complexity of components, has 200 000 circuits each of which has 30 components, i.e. six million components in all. What we are foretelling is that future developments will easily contain today's largest computer on small chips and, with an additional 14 or so other chips, 65 million bits of memory can be added. Even a medium large computer such as the CDC 6500 has a mere eight million bits of internal memory by comparison. All these chips will easily be housed in a device no larger than current pocket calculators and could be readily available in a decade or so. Add on voice recognition chips for input and speech synthesis chips for output, and these future devices will be more sophisticated than anything we have at the present time or could have even dreamed of ten years ago.

Where will these devices lead us? How shall we use such complex devices so small that they can be carried around in our briefcases? The future is certain to be interesting.

Five
How Chips Are Made

One of the most intriguing aspects of the silicon chip is that so many thousands of circuits can be packed onto such a small area. When vacuum tubes were used as the main electronic component in the first era of computers, a great deal of space was required. In the case of ENIAC with its 18 000 tubes it occupied some 3000 cubic feet. Yet, the Fairchild F8 microcomputer of equal computing power takes up only 0.011 cubic feet, some 300 000 times smaller. It is also of interest to record that the F8 consumes 56 000 times *less* power, has a larger main memory, is 10 000 times *more* reliable, and weighs only 0.45 kilograms (1 lb) as opposed to ENIAC's 30 tons. Figure 5.1 compares the Ferranti Mark I Star computer built in 1950 with the Ferranti F100 microprocessor built in 1977. Less cost, less power, less weight, and greater reliability are the additional benefits of current microelectronic technology.

How is it technically possible to create such highly complex devices in so small an area? The actual story itself is an interesting comment on a present-day technology which combines physics, chemistry, photolithography, electronics, and computing science.

The production stages

Broadly speaking, there are three different groups of people, that is companies, involved in the production of working chips. One group designs the circuit pattern which, when realised, functions according to an original specification; for example, a circuit for a camera control system. A second group produces the silicon-based wafers on which the individual chips are formed. A final group receives both the circuit pattern and the silicon wafers and, by a process of photolithography, transfers the circuit design into and onto the silicon wafers.

In the manufacture of a functioning chip, it is helpful to identify four major steps:

The production of the silicon wafers.
The design of the complex circuit pattern.
The photolithographic process.
The testing and packaging of the individual chips.

The production of silicon wafers

It is this process which has given the microprocessor its other name of the "silicon chip". Chip manufacturers often buy wafers of silicon from a company specialising in their production. Their low cost ($10) belies the complexity of their manufacture. The starting point is to reduce raw silicon (Si) from its oxide (SiO_2). Fortunately, for the ecologists of this world, silicon is the most abundant element in the earth's crust. Silicon dioxide, or silica, occurs naturally as sand, quartz and flint stones. We may note that each year 200 000 tonnes are used in castings in silicon steels and aluminium alloys; 20 000 tonnes in polishes, non-stick coatings and resins for silicone compounds; and only 2000 tonnes in semiconductor devices. This is not to say that silicon is the only material which can be used. Gallium arsenide has certain desirable properties and, although more expensive at the present time, it could well be used instead of silicon in the future.

A series of chemical processes purify common sand to 99.999 999 9% pure silicon. Typi-

Figure 5.1 First-generation computers consisting of thousands of valves and miles of interconnecting wire filled entire rooms and required air conditioning. Today, microcomputers of comparable power can be contained on a slice of silicon material some 5 mm square by 1 mm thick. (*Courtesy: Ferranti Ltd*)

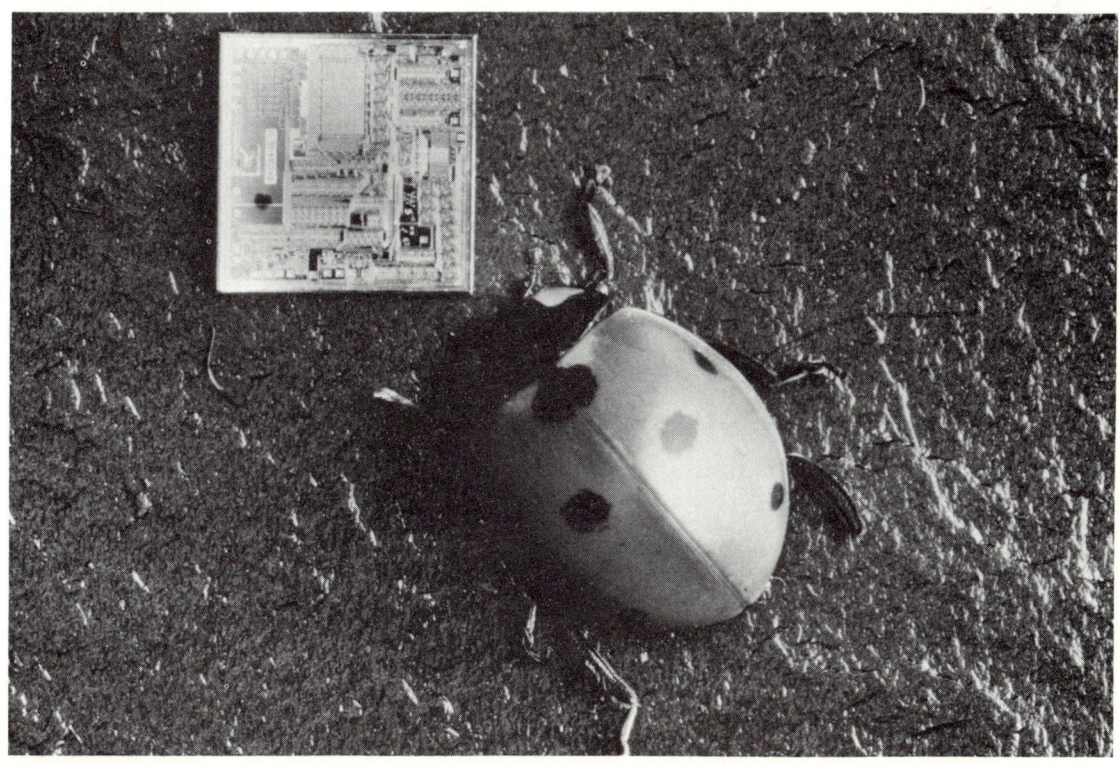

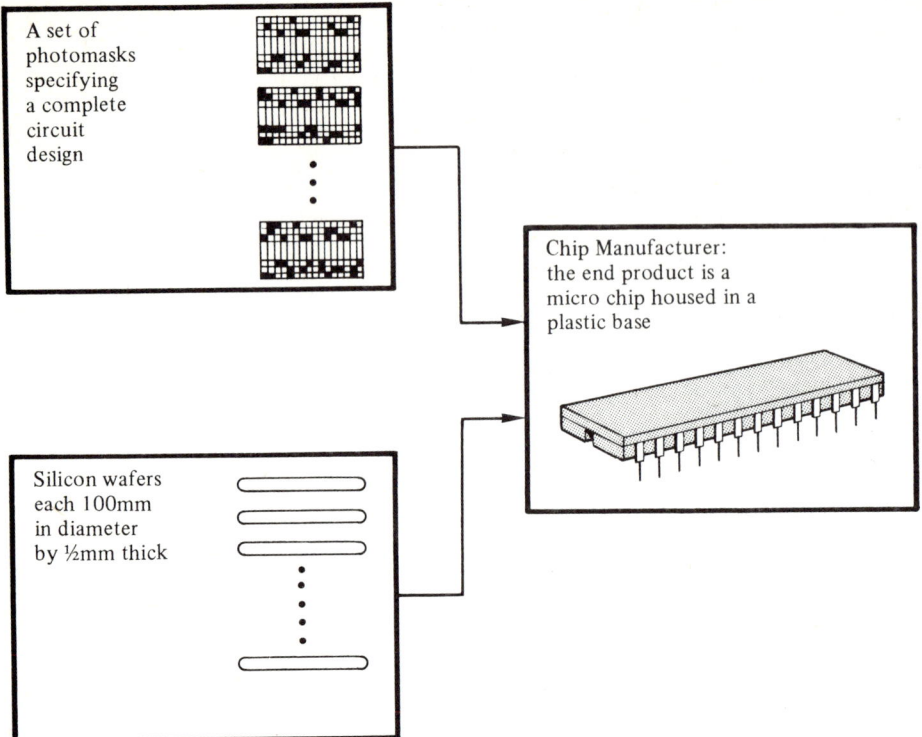

Figure 5.2 Three groups involved in the production of silicon chips.

cally, ten kilograms (22 lbs) is brought up to its melting point of 1420°C in a crucible. An atmosphere of purified inert gas is maintained during this process to prevent oxidisation and undesired impurities from contaminating the melted silicon.

Silicon is known as a *semiconducting material* which simply means that it is neither a good conductor of electricity, such as copper wire, nor a particularly good insulator, such as wood or rubber. Hence, this apparent technical term is really a scientist's way of saying that silicon is neither one thing nor the other.

By their very nature, computers, traditional or micro, are essentially electronic devices and, therefore, silicon must be capable of conducting electrical charges. It is used precisely because its conductivity can be manipulated and controlled. This can be achieved very simply by adding to the purified silicon selected impurities, known as *dopants*, which, in controlled amounts, enable the silicon material to conduct currents in a positive and negative manner, rather like a battery with its negative and positive connections.

One such dopant is the material boron. What occurs when boron is added is that the electronic structure of silicon is altered in such a way that, when a voltage is applied to the doped silicon, a positive charge moves from atom to atom throughout the material. When a controlled amount of phosphorus is added instead of boron, then a different change in the electronic structure takes place so that a negative electrical charge moves through the impaired silicon atomic lattice. Silicon doped with boron results in a positive conductivity and is called a p-type semiconductor material; silicon doped with phosphorus results in a negative conductivity and is called an n-type semiconductor.

A large crystal of doped silicon can be grown by inserting a seed of pure silicon into the melt

Figure 5.3 A single crystal of silicon is grown a metre or so in length by a standard 75 mm or 100 mm in diameter. Rough edges are smoothed and the crystal is cut into ½ mm thick wafers by a thin diamond saw. Hundreds of individual microelectronic chips are formed on each wafer by a process involving photolithography. (*Courtesy: Monsanto Ltd*)

and withdrawing the seed while turning it slowly. The slower the seed is withdrawn, the larger the diameter of the crystal. As the crystal is withdrawn, it solidifies and the rough edges are ground to produce a smooth cylinder of a standard 75 mm (3 inches) or 100 mm (4 inches) in diameter and a metre or so (several feet) in length. This crystal is mounted into a fixture and cut into many slices by a thin diamond saw, each one half a millimetre thick (see figure 5.3).

Each wafer is smoothed on either side by grinding and one side is highly polished to produce an optically flat surface. This final stage is carried out in a very clean atmosphere. The wafers are checked for any defects caused by damage at the polishing stage and then sent off to the chip manufacturer.

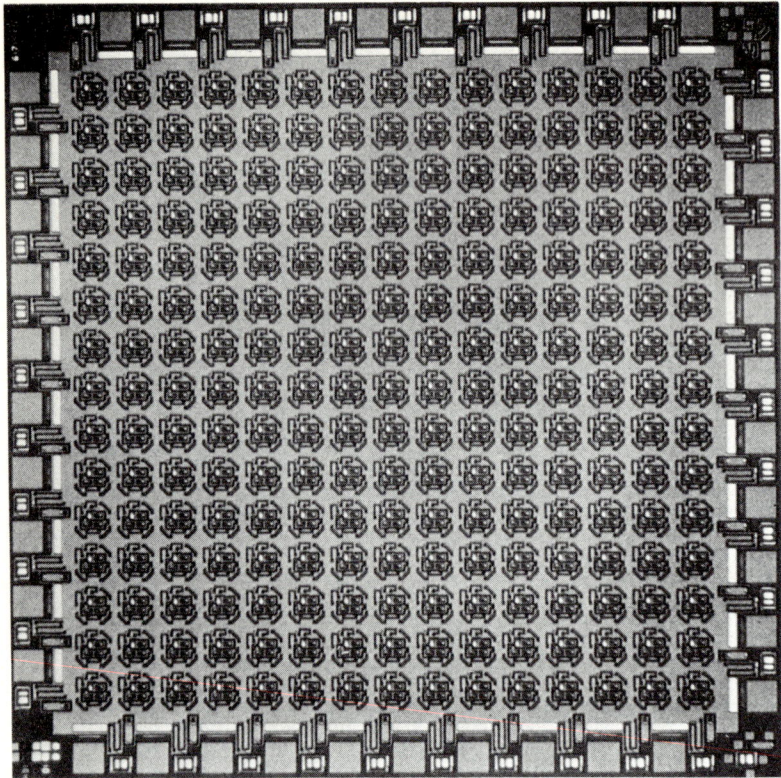

Figure 5.4 An uncommitted logic array (ULA) is seen on the left. It is a prefabricated chip containing an array of logic elements which are complete but not yet linked by metallic connections into any specified circuit pattern. In just one process, these connections can be made to provide a given circuit for a customer, e.g. to control a product such as a camera-control device.

On the right, the metallisation process has been completed so that the chip will function according to a given design of logic.

Circuit design

Circuit designers are responsible for *specifying* the functional characteristics of the microelectronic device. This device may be a conventional microprocessor; a ROM (or PROM or EPROM) or RAM memory chip; a special-purpose chip to control some given system, for example that of an automobile engine or a washing machine; an uncommitted logic array (ULA); or, at a later stage, the required circuit design to be held by a ULA as in the case of the camera-control device (see figure 5.4).

We shall see in the next section that there are several stages (up to eleven in some cases) involved in etching a complete circuit design onto a chip. Some circuits are "pushed" into the silicon base, whilst other circuit patterns are built up layer by layer onto the chip surface thus creating a three-dimensional pattern. Each partial layer of the circuit requires its own pattern. Thus, the circuit designer has to select the required number of layers and the type of processing steps required to realise the final circuit.

After the *specification* designs have been worked out, the circuit designers begin to *design* the actual circuit patterns. Initially, this involves estimating the size and location of each

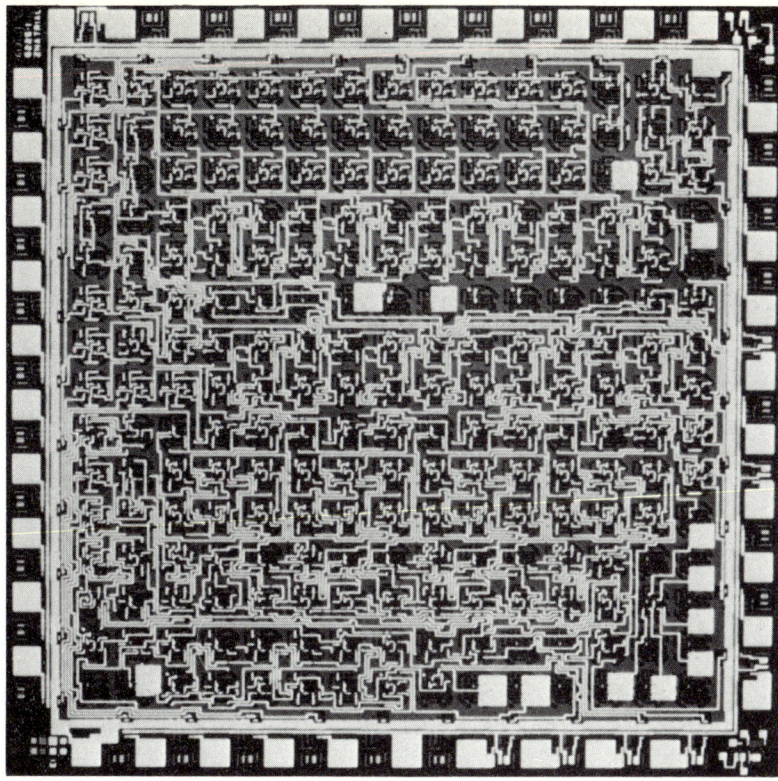

The advantage of ULAs is that, since a single step is required to complete the process, customers receive their chips more cheaply and quickly than when ordering a special custom-built chip. The disadvantage is that customers have to fit the required design into the limits imposed by the fixed-array system so that the eventual circuit configuration may not be the optimum one. (*Courtesy: Ferranti*)

electrical element in the overall circuit pattern. Much of this initial design can be performed with the aid of a computer (computer-aided design, CAD). The computer can simulate the operation of the circuit in a similar way to electronic games which simulate a game of table tennis or star wars. The circuit design can be adjusted until it behaves according to the desired function.

Use of a computer at this stage can be very helpful since it is cheaper, quicker and far more accurate than any other method. The designer can alter a switch or location of any element by typing in a correction at the keyboard of the computer and immediately observing its effect (see figure 5.5). The computer does not perform all the design and the older method of designing many parts of the LSI circuit by hand is still required and is submitted to the computer which will reproduce the design on computer-drawn plots.

The design phase takes a great deal of time depending upon the complexity of the final circuit. The more complex circuitry for the microprocessor can take several years, whereas the basic design of a memory chip which is largely repetitive may take only a few months. It is not unknown, therefore, for a design of a

Figure 5.5 A circuit designer making use of computer aided design (CAD) to create and test a logic design. (*Courtesy: Toshiba*)

specific purpose chip to become out of date because of a change in the industrial firm's production line in which the chip was to have played a part.

The patterns produced by the designers are some 500 times larger than the chip which will eventually contain the circuit patterns (see figure 5.6). These are held in the memory of the computer and transferred to a photographic plate by scanning a computer-controlled light spot across the plate. These patterns, called *reticles*, must be thoroughly checked for any errors and corrected and regenerated until perfect. A reticle pattern, being ten times the size of the final circuit, is reduced to the actual size of the chip by optical methods and then projected onto working plates for use in the manufacturing process. Patterns are sometimes etched onto a chromium film secured on a glass base to make them more durable.

The resulting image of the circuit pattern is reproduced hundreds of times, side-by-side, in a "step and repeat" process onto working plates, called *photomasks*. This is to accommo-

Figure 5.6 Circuit designs are some 500 times larger than the eventual pattern size used on the tiny chip. These larger designs must clearly be thoroughly tested and checked for accuracy before being sent off to the chip manufacturer.
(*Courtesy: National Semiconductor*)

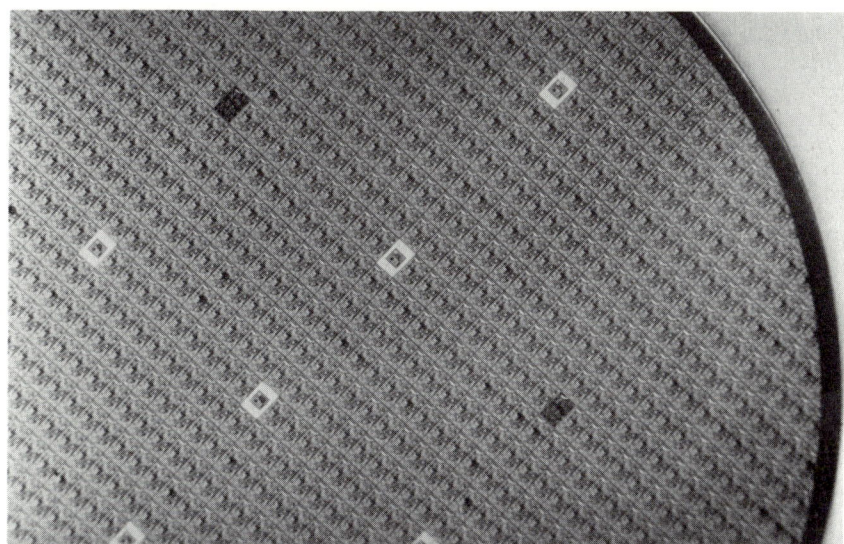

Figure 5.7 A wafer some 100 mm in diameter containing several hundred chips each a mere 5 mm square. Each chip has identical circuit patterns.
(*Courtesy: National Semiconductor*)

date the fact that the silicon wafer of 100 mm in diameter can contain many hundreds of tiny 5 mm (¼ inch) square patterns. A complete set of correct photomasks is the end result of the total design phase of the microelectronic cir- cuit. The plates are delivered to a chip manu- facturer where, in combination with the silicon wafers, the actual usable chip can be fabri- cated.

The manufacture of the silicon chip

The manufacture of integrated circuits, each one measuring some 5 mm square and containing the desired circuit to perform the overall function intended by the circuit designer, requires a high degree of technological expertise. The microelectronic circuit is built up layer by layer, each layer specified by one of the patterns of the photomasks. Since each photomask contains many hundreds of identical patterns, a single wafer at the end of the entire process will contain many hundreds of identical circuits. It

remains for the wafer to be cut up (scribed) into individual chips. But more of this process later. At the moment we need to understand how the various circuit designs can be transferred from the photomask into and onto the silicon wafer.

When the silicon wafers arrive at the chip manufacturer doped, for example, with boron, they are capable of conducting positive-type electrical charges. It is necessary, therefore, to isolate the wafer's base layer from other active electrical areas which will later be built upon its surface. Silicon dioxide is an excellent insulator which can easily be deposited onto a silicon base. This is one of the reasons for selecting silicon as the basic semiconducting material. A wafer of silicon when heated in an atmosphere of oxygen, such as steam, can form a film of silicon dioxide on its surface. Convenient thicknesses can be grown at temperatures in the range of 1000° to 1200°C. For instance, a layer of oxide will form one tenth of a micrometre in one hour at a temperature of 1050°C in an atmosphere of pure oxygen, whereas in an atmosphere of steam and at the same temperature, a layer 0.5 of a micrometre can be deposited.

This oxidisation process is relatively cheap since several hundreds of wafers can be loaded into a quartz "boat" at the same time, each one separated by a few millimetres. The boat, loaded into a quartz tube through which an oxygen-containing gas is passed, is pushed into a furnace whose temperature can be controlled to an accuracy better than one degree. The entire process is often monitored by a process-control computer which regulates the heat of the furnace, the amount of oxygen gas, and the time for which the boat is left in the furnace (see figure 5.8).

The next aim to is etch into the silicon dioxide a pattern such that selected areas of the underlying silicon base or substrate can be exposed. These exposed areas can be doped in a later

Figure 5.8 Many hundreds of wafers can be oxidised at the same time. They are placed in a furnace at a controlled temperature for a given time in an oxygen-containing gas. A thin film of silicon dioxide is deposited on the wafer. Silicon dioxide acts as an excellent insulator.
(*Courtesy: National Semiconductor*)

Figure 5.9 The photographic process

1 The silicon wafer doped to produce, for instance, a p-type base has a film of silicon dioxide deposited onto the surface.
2 A layer of photoresist is deposited over the silicon dioxide.
3 A photomask containing one pattern of the circuit is held above the wafer and exposed to ultraviolet light. Where the light penetrates, the photoresist becomes hardened or fixed. The photoresist not affected by light can be dissolved in a developer solution.
4 The wafer with its photoresist pattern is placed in a developer which dissolves away the masked areas of the photoresist.
5 Next the wafer is placed in hydrofluoric acid which dissolves the exposed areas of silicon dioxide but which does not affect either the hardened photoresist or the underlying silicon base.
By a process of either diffusion or ionisation the exposed areas of silicon can have controlled amounts of dopants introduced into its base according to the original pattern defined by step 3 above.
6 The hardened photoresist can be removed by another chemical process.

By repeating this sequence of events, up to eleven times in some cases and by using different photomasks in step 3, the final circuit design can be etched into the silicon base.

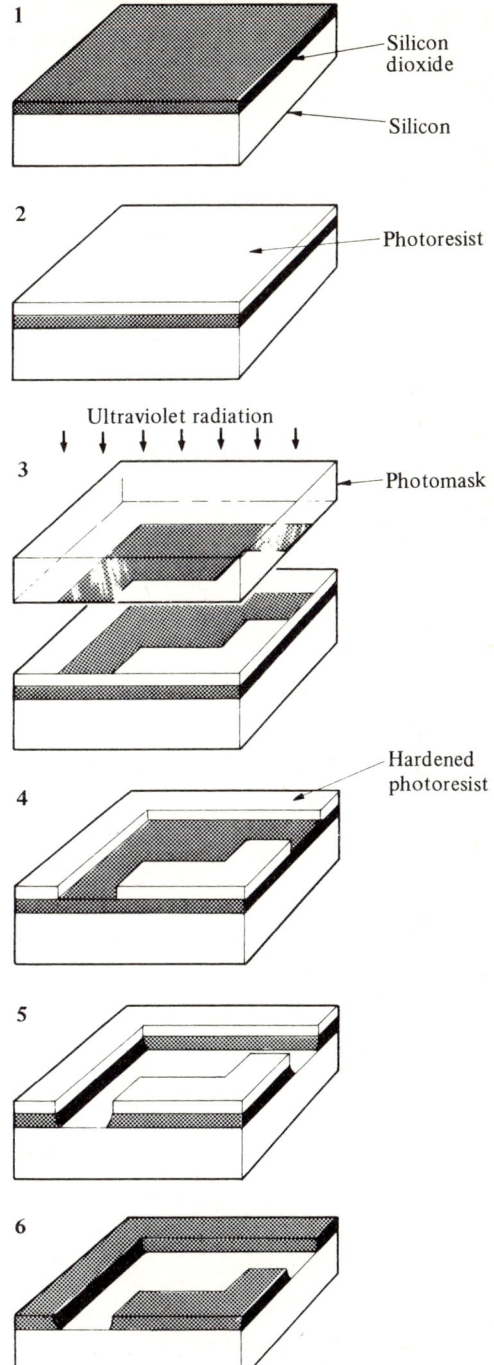

process with phosphorus to create negative-type areas in the p-type substrate. The purpose here is to create a pattern of both p-type and n-type regions in the silicon so that basic electrical areas are formed, thus becoming electrical elements such as transistors, capacitors and resistors. When arranged in organised patterns, these elements form the electronic components which comprise every computer.

Let us see how this is done in one particular case. The starting point is the p-type silicon wafer which has been coated with a layer of insulating oxide (see 1 of figure 5.9). The layer of silicon dioxide is coated with a film of photoresist (see 2 of figure 5.9). Photoresist is a light-sensitive material which is soluble in a certain chemical solvent. Its important property is that, when exposed to ultraviolet light, the photoresist becomes "fixed" and insoluble in the solvent. A photomask pattern (see 3 of figure 5.9) determines those areas which are to be protected (masked). The wafer is then immersed in a solvent, which dissolves the masked areas of photoresist. Later the wafer is immersed in hydroflouric acid which dissolves the exposed areas of silicon dioxide but does not affect the "fixed" photoresist or the underlying silicon base (see figures 4 and 5). The hardened layer of photoresist is removed by another chemical process resulting in step 6 in figure 5.9.

The exposed base of silicon can now be subjected to selective doping with phosphorus and/or boron, creating n-type and p-type regions embedded, for example, in an n-type substrate. By creating islands of p-type material and, in a later processing stage, doping these regions with much smaller n-type regions (see figure 5.10), it is possible to create the electrical elements. Desired patterns of these and other elements can be arranged to give a complete microelectronic circuit which behaves according to the original design specification.

Further coats of photoresist and silicon dioxide can be layered. The oxide is deposited by the process previously described, whereas the photoresist is deposited by placing a drop of the photoresist dissolved in the solvent on top of the wafer and spinning it rapidly. A thin film is spread over the entire wafer in this way and a mild heat treatment helps it to adhere to the surface. Further exposure to ultraviolet light through a second photomask produces a second pattern, and so the process continues. Other layers can be built onto underlying surfaces.

In a final step, a layer of aluminium is formed over the entire surface and the wafer exposed through the final photomask. A warm solution of phosphoric acid selectively attacks the aluminium film, thereby creating a required metallic tracery, to form connections to the circuit elements underneath. A layer of silicon dioxide underneath the aluminium acts as an insulating layer between the two. Figure 5.10 illustrates a series of layers built onto the surface of the silicon substrate which has embedded in it regions of p-type and n-type elements.

The manufacturing process is highly technical and further detail would require a knowledge of microelectronics. But the essential idea is that a three-dimensional pattern is built up by individual layers. Some are buried in the silicon substrate, others laid on the surface. Some surface layers are insulating layers (of silicon dioxide), others form metallic connections. This has given rise to the term *metal-oxide-silicon field effect* transistors (**MOSFET**), which is one of two technologies for creating microelectronic transistors. (The other is called *bipolar*.) The term MOSFET, then, really refers to the three materials used in the fabrication of silicon chips, metal, oxide and silicon.

The atmosphere inside a chip plant must be extremely clean and orderly. Even minute dust particles pose a threat to the tiny chip elements

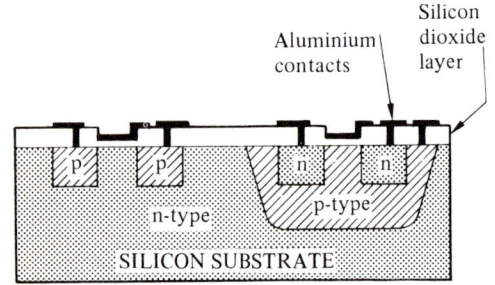

Figure 5.10 Here an n-type silicon substrate has islands of p-type and further n-type regions embedded so that electrical charges can pass through the material to effect the two-state electronic components which comprise computers.

Connections to these circuit elements are made through aluminium conductors deposited over the insulating layer of silicon dioxide at a final stage in the photolithographic process.

Figure 5.11 The *clean room*. Operators wear special clothing to reduce dust being carried into the plant from the outside.
(*Courtesy: National Semiconductor*)

being manufactured. A single particle of dust can cause a defect which will result in the malfunction of the entire circuit. Special clothing is worn to reduce dust particles from outside being carried into the factory. The air is continually filtered and recirculated to keep the dust level at a minimum. A typical chip plant has less than 100 dust particles of a micrometre (a millionth of a metre) or more in diameter per cubic foot of air. A modern hospital by comparison has 10 000 per cubic foot (see figure 5.11).

Photolithography is the key to microelectronic technology. It is used at least once for each layer of the final product. One obvious and important requirement in this process is the exact positioning of each photomask. Machines can adjust the mask to within one or two micrometres. Other techniques involve X-rays, where electron beams have wavelengths measured in nanometres (i.e. thousand-millionths of a metre) rather than in micrometres. They

are, therefore, capable of extremely fine features, and are being developed as possible replacements for existing ultraviolet techniques.

The methods used to inject boron or phosphorus into the silicon base involve either a process of diffusion or ion implantation. In the diffusion process, a boat containing wafers can be placed in a furnace in an atmosphere containing phosphorus. In a temperature of 1100°C, phosphorus (for the creation of n-type regions) can be diffused into the silicon one micrometre in depth in one hour. Thus, controlled amounts of special impurities can be diffused into silicon wherever the silicon has become exposed by some previous etching process.

In ion implantation, impurities are ionised, accelerated by an electric field, and embedded directly into the exposed semiconductor. This method offers much greater control over the quantity and depth of the impurities.

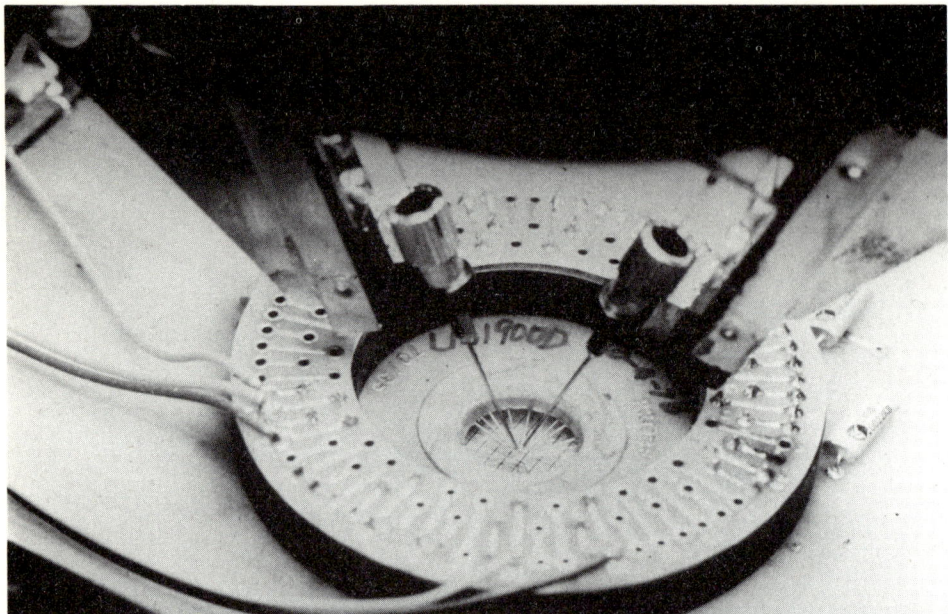

Figure 5.12 After the photolithographic process has implanted into and onto the chips the desired circuit pattern, each chip on the wafer is subjected to an electrical test to determine whether it functions correctly. Frequently, the entire testing process is carried out under computer control. Defective dice (chips) are marked with an ink spot and later rejected.
(*Courtesy: National Semiconductor*)

Testing and packaging

The circuit-manufacturing process ends with a test to determine whether each chip (called a *die*) in the wafer functions correctly. Defective dice are marked with an ink spot to indicate that they should be discarded. A computer-controlled testing machine quickly tests each die circuit and steps on to the next one (see figure 5.12) and, when necessary, performs the inking process without any human intervention. The computer can also keep statistics on the number of good and defective dice as well as the location and nature of the failure of malfunctioning dice. This information can be used to improve the number of good chips (the yield) per wafer.

By scribing between chips and breaking along the lines by passing a roller over the wafer, the individual chips are obtained. Defective dice with ink spots are thrown away and

form a high percentage of the total. Each die must now be "packaged" onto a metal frame and a plastic cover moulded around each chip. Fine gold wires connect the chip to the outside world by being connected to pins at the base of the package. Each unit is subjected to a series of exhaustive tests to make sure that it performs correctly and will continue to do so for a number of years. Figure 5.14 show a wafer being scribed.

The low cost of each chip results from their mass-production. The better the yield per wafer, the lower their unit cost. Other factors which contribute to the final cost are the size of the original wafer which determines the number of chips, the amount of space required for each die, and reduction in the number of defective dice. However, once the chips have been sectioned into individual units, their cost increases substantially because the overall cost is

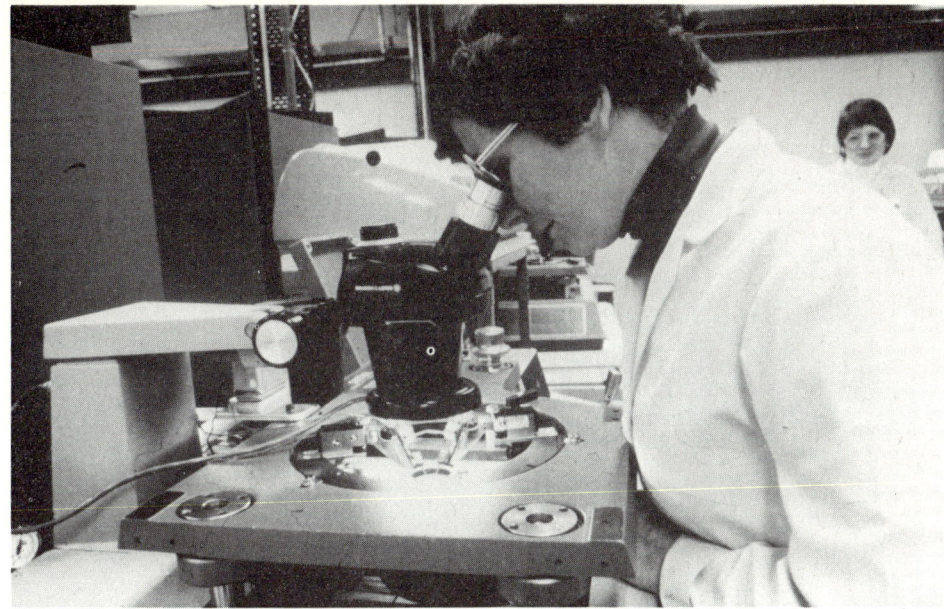

Figure 5. 13 An operator observing and controlling the testing process.
(Courtesy: National Semiconductor)

Figure 5.14 The wafer is scribed along lines and later passed under a roller which breaks along the scribed lines to produce the individual chips.
(Courtesy: National Semiconductor)

Figure 5.15 Individual chips ready for sorting into good and defective chips. These must now be packaged and connected to the metal electrodes on the plastic base and again tested prior to use. (*Courtesy: National Semiconductor*)

no longer shared amongst many. Therefore, the testing and packaging must be automated as far as possible.

According to a set of figures published in *Electronic Digest* (1979), there are 48 manufacturers of chips. These chips are purchased and assembled into functioning microcomputers by some 148 other firms. At the present time, there is only one European microprocessor manufacturer, the UK Ferranti company.

Summary

It may be helpful to summarise the sequence of this somewhat complicated process:

1 *Growing* the silicon crystal.
2 *Polishing* the wafers of silicon.
3 *Oxidisation:* depositing a layer of oxide.
4 *Photoresist and masking:* when exposed to ultraviolet light, the photoresist hardens except in the areas shielded by the mask.
5 *Etching:* the unhardened photoresist is removed by immersion in a solution of developer. The underlying silicon dioxide is removed in a following process by hydroflouric acid which does not affect the hardened photoresist or the silicon base.
6 *Doping:* controlled amounts of impurities are introduced to the exposed silicon surface, either by heating the wafers in a flow of gas containing the desired impurity (phosphorus or boron); or by firing ions of the desired element at the surface of the exposed silicon – ion implantation.

Steps 3, 4, 5 and 6 are repeated up to perhaps 11 times to achieve the required design.

7 *Metallisation:* when the individual components have been completed in the chip, exposed contact points are connected by a tracery of aluminium which can be evaporated onto the surface.
8 *Testing:* defective dice are marked with an ink spot and later rejected when sliced up. Each die is electrically tested to ensure that it works.

9 *Scribing:* after the test, each wafer is scribed or cut into sections. A roller passes over the scribed wafer causing the lines to break and thus yield individual chips.

10 *Bonding and packaging:* good chips are selected by hand and mounted onto their plastic carriers.

Six
Using Chips

It has been estimated that there are at least fifteen electric motors in the average household. A similar if not greater number of household devices will contain microprocessors or micro-computers before too long. Currently, we already have electronic washing machines, microwave ovens, pocket calculators, digital watches, domestic television games, personal computer systems, electronic learning aids, sewing machines, and video tape recorders.

In the public area at large, microelectronics are used in petrol pumps, taxi meters, public-house gaming devices, navigational aids, lime-stone quarrying, military equipment, communications equipment, spacecraft, etc. The micro will invade many more everyday products, many of which we will not even be aware of. The number of potential application areas is vast. Some 20 000 applications have already been identified.

Where do we begin? One microcomputer can cost £50, another over £5000. They cannot both achieve exactly the same results, otherwise the more expensive one would never sell. So what is the difference? This depends upon the application. A £50 micro on a single chip is not going to be suitable for processing and storing the medical records for a general practitioner or for any general commercial and data processing task such as job or client costing. On the other hand, a £5000 microcomputer system controlling a taxi-meter makes nonsense when a much cheaper system involving one or more chips can perform all the required functions.

Since this is an introductory text, we have classified two broad types of micros. The first is the chip computer comprising one or more chips; the other is the multi-board micocomputer complete with input and output devices and some form of auxiliary storage device.

The chip-level micro is used in general industrial or process control environments where some form of measuring, control, calculating, display, monitoring or detection device is used. The advantages of using microelectronics in these situations is that they are smaller, cheaper and more reliable than existing electro-mechanical devices performing the same function. Thus, they can be used in existing products such as security devices, smoke detectors, cash registers and cash dispensers, communications equipment, typewriters, lift controls, and so forth, as well as in a whole new range of products, for instance word processors, electronic toys and teaching aids, and meters to record telephone charges and to report system failures. It is in this broad industrial environment that the last two British governments have sponsored training programmes because it is clear that industry is to become more and more dependent upon microtechnology.

In data processing, microcomputer systems provide more reliable and up-to-date information on which management decisions can be based, potentially resulting in a more efficient business. Less time need be spent by staff in performing routine jobs which can be carried out more efficiently by the micro-system. Staff will then have more time to extend a personal service to customers and to clients. However, the larger and more expensive multi-board microcomputer systems are necessary for many of these applications, or some form of portable communications device linking a local shop or office to a centralised computer centre.

The purpose of this chapter is to highlight a few areas where microprocessor technology can provide assistance. This may well mean a change in the future organisation of established practices. It is to be hoped that this chapter may encourage those responsible for making decisions to realise the potential of micro-computers and, at least, to investigate the possible use of this high technology in their own fields.

Examples are given of applications in industrial processes and products, in public and commercial organisations, and in small businesses.

The motor car

There are three main applications areas for the motor car industry. First, there is the basic engine monitor, a micro device which checks fuel flow, resulting in maximum engine efficiency and thereby reducing fuel consumption and emission of pollutants. The system in use on the Jaguar saloon Series III 4.2 litre engine (for export only in 1980) and developed by Lucas Industries can be taken as the kind of system which will appear in some new cars over the next two years.

Lucas claims that the system cuts fuel consumption by at least 25% by ensuring that all fuel is actually burnt. Pollution from exhaust fumes is non-existent since all that comes out from the exhaust is hot air! A small micro generates electrical pulses through a 1K ROM fuel scheduling program. These pulses are applied to solenoids which open and close the fuel injector system. The duration of the pulses determines the amount of fuel to be injected.

The input to the program comes from two main sources – air flow and engine speed. The program controls the correct mixture of air to fuel. Although this may appear simple, fuel flow varies according to a wide range of conditions, such as starting up, warming-up period, idling, full car load, rapid acceleration, and rapid deceleration. All these variants are detected and controlled by the ROM program.

A second area is the provision of information for the driver. All cars have a speedometer, a fuel gauge, indicator lights for ignition and oil pressure; others have a clock, water temperature gauge and a rev counter. A micro system linking all these together can process the various information and compute results; for example, the average fuel consumption for a journey, the average car speed, the current time and the elapsed time since the start of a journey, the number of miles or kilometres to go to some predetermined destination, the estimated time of arrival, the driving range on remaining fuel, the engine temperature, and so on. Additional devices could provide information such as the outside and inside temperature, the state of the battery, and a reminder alarm.

Future devices could prevent a car from skidding or even from crashing. BMW, for instance, plans to use a micro-based system to prevent the brakes from locking the wheels. The system checks the speed of each wheel and compares them with each other to ensure that the disparity is not greater than a predetermined limit. Anti-crash devices consist of a small microwave radar in the front of the car which can register solid objects ahead and determine their speed. The device can then adjust the speed of its own car accordingly. If the object ahead is stationary then the car will stop, making it impossible to go on so that the driver could not crash the car even if he wanted to.

A third application area, already undergoing tests in the Rhine by Volkswagen in conjunction with the West German Ministry of Research & Technology, is designed to guide the driver to his destination by the quickest and least congested route. At the start of a journey, the driver "keys in" his destination and follows his normal route. LISA, the navigation system, collects information on traffic hold-ups from police traffic control systems interspersed along the route as well as from information transmitted by road signs. This information, processed by LISA, tells the driver via a simplified map on a graphic display inside the car where and when to turn off to avoid traffic jams. Clearly, this system will take many years before it is in use generally in most countries.

Telephone systems

The Post Office in the UK installed some microprocessor telephones at Heathrow Airport and Victoria Station in 1980. These have pushbuttons in place of the more conventional dials and can make contact direct with 89 countries. A feature of this system is that it allows users to put money in on credit. The amount inserted is shown on a LED display (light emitting diode). As the call begins, the credit reduces by 2 pence decrements. Ten seconds before the money runs out, the display requests more money and provides an audible bleep for non-sighted persons. If the call ends before the credit runs out, the caller has the choice of placing another call by pressing a "follow-on" button or of requesting unused coins to be returned. A second feature is that the microprocessor automatically informs the PO of any major defect in the system, making repairs a faster process.

Voice recognition

It is not only in public and domestic areas that the micro will become commonplace but also in most areas of work. Employees of the Standard Chartered Bank which deals with foreign exchange use a voice recognition system. They first of all "teach" the system to recognise their voice patterns and thereafter can enter information into the system via a microphone. The voice sounds are reproduced on a display, allowing the speaker to verify the accuracy of his input.

Robotics and control

Paint spraying can easily be performed by robotic devices controlled by micros. First, an experienced human sprayer teaches his hand and arm movements to a micro system simply by going through his normal procedure. Every

movement is recorded by the system. Later, the same object, a chair, a car body or whatever, can be automatically sprayed by a microcontrolled machine provided the object is placed in the same position as for the human sprayer.

A carpet factory in Yorkshire uses a microcontrolled machine to pattern plain tufted carpets. The machine contains the information about the pattern and controls the colouring process. Another system based on micro sensors is trying to determine once and for all whether Loch Ness really does have its monster. The sensors will beam their signals up to a communications satellite where they will be bounced to a switching centre in Houston, Texas; from there they are transmitted to Toulouse in Western France for processing. This aspect of telecommunications is developed further in Chapter 8.

Within medicine, micros are being developed to aid severly handicapped people. A prototype robotic micro-controlled arm for instance has been developed at Queen Mary College, London. It can be operated by a patient able to hold, for example, nothing but a stick in his mouth. By pressing given function buttons, the pre-programmed arm can perform a variety of actions.

A small micro-chip embedded in the heart of a human being and linked to an artificial pacemaker can sense the pulses of the heart's own natural pacemaker and pass these on to the artificial one and control the pace at which it needs to operate. Non-micro-controlled artificial pacemakers can simply pace the heart at a regular 70 beats, regardless of the individual's activity such as lying down or running for a bus.

Farming

A farm is a small business although requirements are not exactly the same as those of most small businesses. Farm businesses tend to be orientated towards cash analysis at cash time and not at invoice time. Consequently, double entry systems are virtually non-existent. This is not a problem for a microcomputer system since general-purpose systems can be made flexible by a program tailor-made to suit a given farming community. Farmers need more than just an accounting system, and a typical farm data processing system could handle three different tasks.

First, it would handle all the financial considerations and in the way that the farmer is used to, but in addition it would also provide more information than the farmer normally would have from his own manual accounting system. Secondly, management reports are produced regularly in order to provide such details as milk yields, and the harvest of a particular crop. Thirdly, such routine tasks as payroll can be performed. One system for under £5000 comprises a microprocessor, visual display unit, printer and twin floppy discs. However, the application programs have to be bought separately but include payroll, accounting, arable crop farming, and dairy management.

Microcomputer control systems are also under development to measure the milk yield, control the food dispensers, and measure the weight and the temperature of each cow which can be individually "recognised" by the system through a signal transmitted from a transponder contained in the collar of the cow. This system can also provide management information so that each cow can have its milk yield reported. Those cows yielding more or less than the average can be listed together with those whose temperature is higher than normal.

The estate agent

An estate agency lives or dies by its mailing system. Information about properties for sale is stored in a microcomputer system along with the requirements of prospective buyers. By matching what is required and what is for sale, it is possible to produce a list of properties for a given client. A computer system can provide much greater efficiency, leaving staff to concentrate on the personal service when face to face with clients. One system consisting of a microprocessor, VDU and printer with floppy disc storage is on offer for about £12 000. Although the actual hardware costs only about £5000, the rest is for the application programs, training, documentation and tailoring the application programs to individual requirements.

The general practitioner

There are 27 000 general practitioners in the UK, all of whom are self-employed businessmen concerned with health care. They are paid by the State under the National Health Service. This payment system has evolved into a highly complex task over the years since 1944 when the service was introduced. Some 100 forms are involved on which GPs claim separate fees and allowances. This is the business side, but the clinical practice is even more open to computerisation as we have already seen (in chapter 2, pp. 16–17). Some micro-based systems have been developed since 1978 and can provide a complete register of all patients according to sex and age; and registers such as those patients at risk say from obesity or smoking and, similarly, all patients with a given illness such as high blood pressure or diabetes. A summary of each patient is provided so that, on entry to the doctor's surgery, the doctor has all necessary and vital facts at the touch of a button. Lists of patients requiring vaccinations (for example, all children under one year) and women requiring cervical cancer tests can also be listed by the system with little trouble. Finally, the system can cope with the business side of the practice by checking the accounts and determining whether all fees have been claimed.

Thus, a microcomputer can help in three areas: practice accounting, patients' case histories, and clinical administration. Systems on offer vary from £2000 to £24 000. The larger group practices could well afford to at least investigate the possibilities. Getting hold of the information and entering it into the system in the first place is not so daunting a task as it may seem. Patient questionnaires can help a great deal and, once these details have been entered, they can be printed out, checked for accuracy, and then printed out according to any of the lists given above.

Retail ordering

UniChem, an independent pharmaceutical wholesaler, distributes a large range of products (approximately 25 000) to some 5000 independent dispensing chemists throughout England, Scotland and Wales. A fleet of some 300 vans from twelve branches scattered throughout the UK deliver urgently needed drugs and other products to pharmacies up to three times a day. In the past it was necessary for UniChem to telephone each client about one hour before the scheduled departure time of each delivery vehicle.

In mid-1978 a new ordering concept was introduced which has so far been adopted by over 1500 chemists. The new service, called PROSPER$_x$, is based upon a small hand-held terminal which provides the facility for electronic order collection and transmission. The portable terminal has 4K of RAM store powered by internal rechargeable batteries, and is capable of storing over 250 separate order lines.

Additional features of the PROSPER$_x$ system includes price labels containing not only the unique six-digit product code, and the retail price, but also information useful to the retailer e.g. purchase date to enable stock rotation, unique shop identifier code, etc.

With each PROSPER$_x$ system comes a complete set of plasticised shelf edge labels which are updated on a regular basis. These labels stick on the shop fixtures and contain unique product code information as well as product description. There is space for stock re-order level and re-order quantity details to be added.

Once a pharmacist begins to use PROSPER$_x$, UniChem produce a detailed report of his purchases each month, and every three months

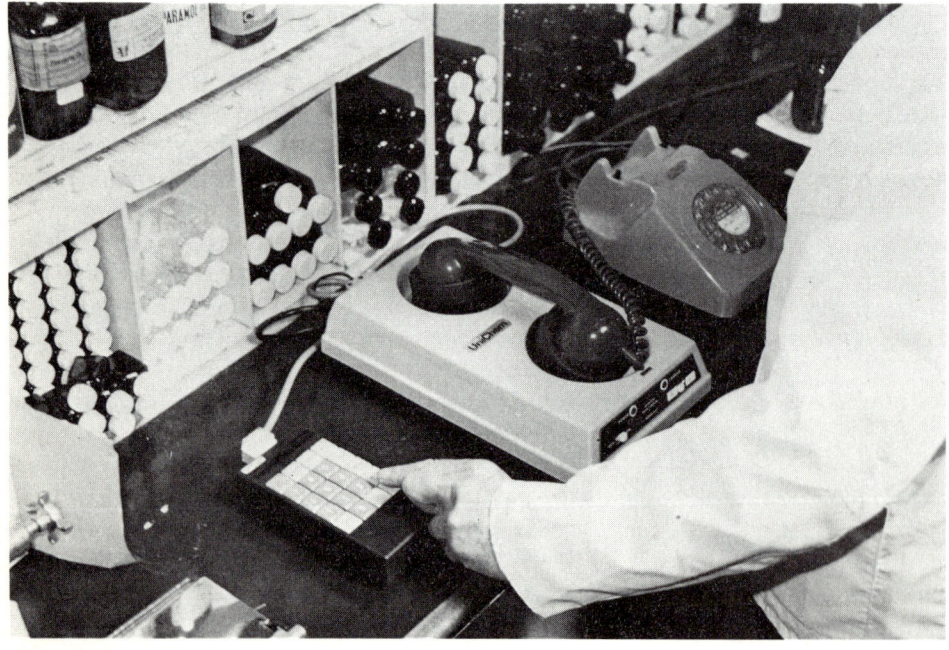

Figure 6.1 Here the chemist may check the current stock levels and enter re-ordering information directly into the system via the special data pad input device. Later this device is linked to a central computer system by normal Post Office speech lines. The chemist's work is reduced from about 30 minutes to an average of 30 seconds, thereby freeing him for his more specialised work. (*Courtesy: UniChem*)

this is analysed to produce a management report detailing the last quarter's purchases, compared to the previous four quarter's transactions. In this way UniChem's computers are able to highlight sales trends as well as produce stock control information to be written onto the shelf edge labels.

The ordering procedure begins with the assistant in the chemist's shop "keying in" the product code and order quantity for the items required. Each product code contains a check digit to reduce the number of input errors. Check digit errors are rejected by the terminal and the assistant is warned by an audible alarm. All valid product codes and order quantities are stored in RAM and may be displayed at any time.

Once the complete order has been entered, the terminal is linked to an ordinary telephone via an *acoustic coupler* which converts digital noughts and ones into analogue format suitable for transmission over the public telephone net-

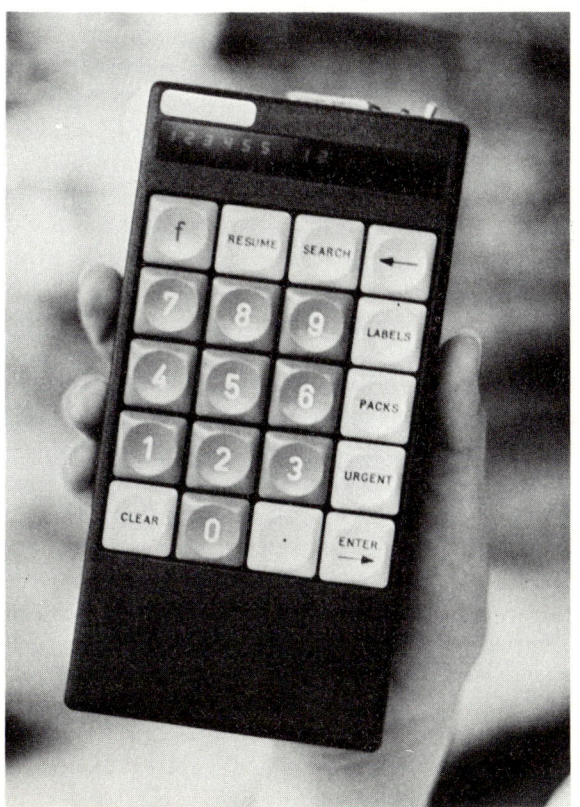

work at the rate of 30 characters a second. At UniChem's Data Processing Centre a similar device is used to convert data from analogue back into digital format before passing it to one of the computers used to gather order information. If "noise" on the line causes corruption of the data being transmitted, the computer will automatically request that that piece of information be sent again. This "Sorry repeat that again" procedure is carried out automatically without the pharmacist being aware of it. Once all of the data has been successfully received, the order-gathering computer acknowledges the fact and causes the terminal to display a "Send Done" message. If however, the number of "Sorry, repeat that again" actions exceeds a specified number, then the overall validity of the order is in doubt, and the order-gathering computer causes the transmission to be terminated, the data purged from its storage system, and the message "Send Error" to be displayed on the terminal, thus warning the pharmacist that his order will have to be sent again, hopefully this time on a better-quality line.

Once the order has been successfully received by the order-gathering computer, it is passed to another machine that performs the Order Processing. The end result is an invoice transmitted over a permanently leased telephone line to be printed at the branch that will be delivering the customer's goods. It is then assembled, and despatched by van, often within fifteen minutes of its receipt at the Computer Centre.

Advantages of the PROSPER$_x$ system of electronic ordering are first, that the pharmacist may transmit his order any time, day or night, throughout the year. This makes ordering more convenient for him, and items are not forgotten as often happens when ordering by telephone. Secondly, the statistics that are produced by the system enable the retailer to reduce over-ordering and out-of-stock situations, thus maintaining a better and, therefore, more profitable balance of purchases to sales. Finally, price stickers produce reliable, easy-to-use information which also enhances the "professional" image given to the retailer's customers.

To summarise, the independent pharmacist today does all of the jobs from Managing Director, down to making the tea. His main role, however, is that of decision maker. UniChem's PROSPER$_x$ system provides the pharmacist with reliable, quick information upon which to base his day-to-day business decisions. Such a system is indicative of what will happen in many areas of the retail trade.

Salesmen

Other systems of a similar nature are in use. For example, Smedley-HP Foods have a system which speeds up order processing and data collection from its 150 salesmen. In the past, each salesman wrote the customer's order details on a separate five-part pre-printed form. The top copy was posted to the computer centre, one was kept for the salesman's own reference, the others sent off to the appropriate warehouse or factory. Today, each salesman has a portable terminal with a standard numerical layout and a few special function buttons. Via an acoustic coupler it can be linked to any telephone.

Where it differs from the Prosper system is that the salesman receives a human voice response on contacting the Smedley-HP computer centre. The salesman dials the PO Freephone number and enters a unique identity number. A voice acknowledges the number and the salesman is able to enter the order data. The system will repeat vocally each detail after it has been keyed-in to check on the accuracy. Most salesmen, however, once they have become familiar with the system prefer to select a bleep response as an alternative to voice response.

Any mistakes such as entering discontinued lines or non-existent pack sizes will produce a voice-prompt from the system stating the occurrence of an error and preventing the information from being accepted. A cancel key, one of the function buttons, can erase an otherwise valid entry or, if necessary, an entire order. A repeat key enables the salesman to receive part or all of a recording. Along with the order itself, the salesman enters the customer's account number and delivery instructions so that the order can be processed by the computer centre the moment the terminal is disconnected from the telephone.

The advantages of both systems are obvious. They are faster, more accurate, far more efficient, and, in the case of the chemist shop system, reduce the work load of the staff so that they have more time to attend to customers. In the case of Smedley-HP, there has been a further saving annually of many thousands of pounds on the erstwhile pre-printed order forms.

But a much more important point is that both systems demonstrate the linking together of computing power and the telephone system. The first requires information or data to process; the second, provides a means of getting that data into the computer system as quickly as possible. With satellite communications, information can be passed between countries and even continents. One school-boy who had a program to write as part of his homework was able to use his father's office terminal in London which was linked to a computer centre in America. While waiting for his father at the office, he typed in the program, had it processed by the computer in Texas, and the printed results bounced back via satellite communications to the printing device attached to the terminal. This may not be the usual purpose of such devices but it does illustrate the way things are going to go. Telecommunications and the cheapness of computing power via microprocessors and microcomputers are the two technologies which will alter the way in which society handles information over the next few years.

Seven
Microcomputers in Schools

It is encouraging to find that some of the most enthusiastic users of microcomputers are secondary schools. Since the main inheritors of the microelectronic world are now at school, careful nurturing of young people's knowledge will help them to cope with the technology which their elders have created.

In 1977, a mere handful of schools possessed a microcomputer, typically the rather primitive single board variety, usually introduced by an electronic enthusiast from the teaching staff. By 1980, many hundreds of schools had installed comparatively sophisticated micros with many hundreds more contemplating a purchase. Schools are typical of the growing generation able to purchase on-site computing facilities. Formerly, the majority of schools could not think of such an expenditure – even a modest minicomputer of the 1970s would have cost over £30 000 plus annual maintenance. Consequently, schools had to resort to a variety of means in order that student's programs would be processed by a real computer. This resulted in many frustrations for both school staff and students as well as for the computer centre personnel *running* schools' work on their computer system. One hard-pressed CSE examining board in Computer Studies was even forced into the ludicrous position of accepting "programs" for examination projects which had been written on special program forms but which had never been near a computer. Who could tell whether the programs were correctly written or not?

The past few years have changed all that. A modest microcomputer can be purchased for £2000 or so, a cost within the reach of most schools even if they have to resort to "summer fayres" and sponsored walks.

Microcomputers can be useful in a variety of ways but most important is that a future generation will emerge with at least some practical knowledge and experience of microcomputer technology.

Uses within education

There are several ways in which a microcomputer can enhance everyday secondary education.

1 It provides the necessary computer facilities for learning the art of computer programming and for processing programs for Computer Studies examinations at CSE and O-level, and Computing Science at A-level. Also pupils gain practical experience in the use of a microcomputer.

2 In addition to the above, A-level students not only learn *high-level programming* in, for example, BASIC or FORTRAN, but also *low-level programming*. Furthermore, the existence of a microcomputer will enable these students to develop a more detailed knowledge of the hardware aspects of microtechnology and design.

3 Subjects such as Electronics and Physics can benefit enormously by the provision of cheap electronic hardware for practical experiments.

4 Many subjects are moving away from theory to a more pragmatic approach. There is a need for models of the real world. Computer Assisted Learning (CAL) programs can provide such models especially in subjects as Geography, Economics, and Social Sciences.

5 The computer is an ideal tool to teach many routine aspects of a syllabus, again via pre-

written computer programs. Currently, teachers find little time to devote to students who miss certain lessons because of illness or who have slow learning ability, as for example those who suffer from dyslexia. What is needed in these situations is almost a one-to-one ratio between student and teacher. The computer, on the other hand, is always available for such individual teaching.

6 Other handicapped children such as the blind, the physically disabled needing special teaching, the mentally handicapped, and so on, can be helped to learn more quickly and thoroughly if part of the routine learning can be provided by computer teaching machines. For instance, one Apple microcomputer system is used to teach deaf children to talk. They learn more quickly from the computer than they do from even the most attentive teacher.

7 Finally, much of a school's administration could be performed by a little micro system tucked away in the secretary's office. Class lists in age, name or sex order can be quickly produced. Mailing lists for parents; an aid to time-tabling; stock control of essential school equipment or the tuck shop; menus for school dinners; room allocation; control and issue of library books; fees for children in the private school sector; are some of the ways in which the microcomputer can help. However, it is important that the administration system is kept entirely separate from the teaching system, otherwise the inevitable conflict about priorities will follow.

At the present time, most schools will be using micros with varying degrees of success in only one area, that of Computer Studies at CSE and O-level. A few may be using their machines with some effect in one or more of the other areas, but these are the exceptions rather than the norm.

Computer assisted learning

The main impact of computers in schools lies with CAL. According to the context in which this term is used, CAL has several meanings. Here, CAL is taken to mean the teaching of part of a given subject through the medium of pre-written computer programs. These programs may be used by an entire class at one time or by individuals at separate times. The programs are so constructed that they take a student or a class of students step-by-step through the learning process.

Some programs will be simple (yet still effective) such as providing extra tuition in the art of arithmetic. A student who has difficulty with multiplication and division, for example, can gain extra tuition via the computer. A program will present an exercise and await the answer from the student. If it is correct, a "friendly" program will offer some praise and move onto another exercise, perhaps a slightly harder one. But if the answer is incorrect, the program will pass a comment and ask the student to try again. Usually, two or more attempts at the answer are allowed, after which the program will provide the correct answer and offer some explanation as to how the answer is arrived at. After a complete session, the program will display the total score of correct answers and issue some appropriate comment.

Even these apparently simple CAL programs involve a great deal of time for the person writing the program. More complicated CAL programs may involve many man-years of work. Such an example is the DIET package developed by David Lawrence for Home Economics. In his 1972 introduction to the package he says:

"The study of nutrition involves amongst other things the intuitive ability to be able to prescribe adequate diets for various types of people over given periods of time. Moreover, in some cases, not only the nutritional aspect of this exercise but also the financial one must be considered by the student. Since the amount of arithmetic needed to accurately evaluate such a problem is formidable and confusing, and since a student can not reasonably be expected to be thoroughly familiar with actually providing food and budgeting in such a wide range of situations, the problem is an ideal case for computer simulation.

DIET is not intended in any way to supplant the teacher: the programs provide a means of giving the students a wealth of simulated practical experience of the subject.

The user of a DIET program is invited to suggest a diet and the computer then assesses it from several viewpoints. Currently, the programs cover between them the following aspects of this general situation: analysis of the nutritional content of food; adequacy of diet under conditions of normal health; nutritional needs of individuals, groups and families; vegetarianism; budgeting; continuous cost control; bulk purchasing; comparison of effective price of nutrients. It is hoped that, by going into the topic in this depth, DIET will be a means of conveying to the students a real understanding of the concepts involved."

An interesting point is that neither the teacher nor the student needs to have any knowledge of computer programming or computer science in order to make use of the package. However, clearly written documentation must accompany such packages outlining in detail exactly how to use it. DIET makes use of a data-base file of prices of various foods. One difficulty in this age of inflation is to keep this file up-to-date.

Despite almost ten years of teacher involvement in CAL, very few comprehensive and useful packages exist. Clearly, teachers have not the time to invest in such work. The impetus for large-scale programs must come from the commercial world. A huge educational industry is required which is ready to invest capital, manpower and the necessary marketing expertise. Experienced teachers from the various disciplines are the right people to be involved in the writing of programs and will probably have to be seconded into the industry, thereby helping to relieve the unemployment problem for many young teachers fresh from Colleges of Education.

Another development upon which the ultimate success of CAL rests is in the use of graphical display, preferably in colour. Techniques including animated diagrams and images and diagram build-up will add a completely new dimension to the somewhat restricting alphabetical communication between student and computer. Cost is a major factor which precludes widespread use of graphics today.

Hopefully, within five years, hardware and software prices will fall sufficiently to be within the grasp of most schools.

Future systems

As human beings, we communicate through voice, gesture and touch. Current communication between computer and humans is restricted in the main to keyboard input and visual display of alphabetic characters. Future systems will permit voice input and output, touch and even gestures. An example will help to illustrate this point. It includes use of the video disc mentioned in chapter 4.

Imagine you wish to remove the front hub from your bicycle. You can call up, by voice, from your optical video disc attached to the home computer, the details for *bicycle maintenance*. Displayed on the screen will be various parts of the bicycle. One of these will be the front hub. By *touching* this part with your finger, the computer is "told" to present details of the front hub. If a tool needs to be used with which you are not familiar, then again by touching this tool on the screen the computer is informed that details concerning the use of this tool are required before proceeding any further. Later on, if other tools are used, then the computer will assume that details of their use are also required.

Touch panels are ideal for school work and eliminate the use of light pens which have proved to be unreliable in classroom use in the States. Amazingly, a finger has the ability to pinpoint accurately to 1/1000 of an inch when the ball of the finger is rotated. Plastic touch panels do not become dirty or greasy from constant touch unlike the more common glass panels of cathode ray tube screens.

Other future communication devices will recognise and respond even to our gestures. We shall be able to say: "Put *that* over *there*," and by defining *that* and *there* by pointing, the computer system will move the defined objects about on a screen. This will have a direct impact in the area of computer graphics. If this sounds somewhat far-fetched, let me add that I have seen prototype devices at work and commercial companies will have them in common use before the end of the 1980s.

They work on a magnetic principle. When pointing to a screen, the user has a small magnetic device, small enough to fit into a watch, cuff-link or a ring. This emits a magnetic force which can be received by the computing device. In this way, the spot on the screen at which you are pointing can be plotted by x and y coordinates.

Other systems under development have the ability to track eye movements. In the case of a severely handicapped person with only eyesight intact, he or she need only look at a screen or a set of *function* buttons in order to initiate their activity. Such buttons could open and close doors, even to let the cat in and out, ring bells for an alarm, switch certain domestic appliances on or off, turn to another page of a book displayed on the screen, and so forth. One eye-tracking device works on a magnetic principle similar to the above. The magnetic emitter is worn on a cap and the x and y coordinates displaced to such a degree that the eye itself can be plotted. Another device emits a harmless laser beam which can be reflected off the eye and back to the device, thereby plotting the angle of the eye.

When all these developments come together, that is the commercial interest, low-cost graphical equipment, video discs, touch panels, voice recognition and speech, and gesture devices, CAL will begin to have far-reaching implications for education as a whole. But we cannot expect too much before the end of this decade. In the meanwhile, the current situation is much more mundane. Let us consider some of the problems which you as a microcomputer owner have to face, whether you are a teacher, lecturer, student or, indeed, a small business manager.

Having your own micro

Having your own computer on-site to be used at your own time, rather than having to rely on the whim of a computer centre, a computer bureau or a friendly local company, has an instant appeal. However, as owner you have to take on certain responsibilities previously shouldered by the computer personnel at the centre. A few of these management tasks are listed below. Some may seem trivial until you are forced to face the problem yourself.

1 Decide on which microcomputer manufacturer to select and what hardware and software are needed. There are over 150 different manufacturers to choose from. Each one will offer that something different.

2 Assemble the hardware units once they have arrived. This may be carried out by the agency which supplies the components.

3 The hardware units and the software have to be tested to ensure that they work correctly once they are in your possession.

4 Suitable housing for the equipment has to be thought about in advance. Is there sufficient space for you to work in?

5 Is the documentation provided by the manufacturer simple enough and comprehensive enough to be followed? In practice, very few manufacturers supply adequate documentation so that you as manager may well have to prepare your own. This implies that you have taken the necessary time to teach yourself how to use the system.

6 Timetable the use of the system (particularly relevant in schools).

7 Time must be set aside to oversee and organise the use of the system.

8 Provide measures for the security and safekeeping of the equipment.

9 Provide measures for the security and safekeeping of the programs and data files – one copy of each is not enough. Two or three copies are the norm.

10 If the manufacturer has a "user group", take time off to attend meetings.

11 What are your maintenance arrangements when faults and malfunctioning occur? If you can, identify the fault (not an easy task to a complete novice) and arrange for the component to be returned. In the meantime, have you a spare component so that the system can continue to function? If not, have you considered the impact on your business or teaching environment if you are without the micro for days at a time?

Incidentally, where is the supplier or manufacturer? Does the firm lie within easy reach so that returning faulty equipment does not require a major effort?

Arrange for periodic maintenance check-ups.

12 Have you the time to keep up-to-date with other developments your manufacturer is exploiting?

13 Are you providing time to take note of falling stock levels of ribbons and printer paper? Who will re-order such stocks?

14 Have you considered involving other colleagues in order to avoid being regarded as a "micro-ham"?

Eight
The Coming Tide

Of one fact we can be certain – microelectronic devices are here to stay. Furthermore, the microelectronic industry has only just begun. Even more powerful micro-chips are emerging, microprocessors are becoming more powerful, storage chips are of increasing capacity, and developments in the transmission of information more sophisticated resulting in an information revolution. In this chapter, we shall consider some of the implications which we shall all have to face in the coming years. For more information, there are many books entirely devoted to this subject (see page 67 particularly).

An unprecedented technological impact

It was in 1971 that the first microprocessor on a chip was offered to the world – the INTEL 4004. Other manufacturers may debate Intel's achievement, but for the world at large, microprocessors became a reality in the early 1970s. At that time, very few people, even computer scientists, could claim any intimate knowledge of this microelectronic device. Yet by 1980, a mere ten years after its appearance, this phenomenon had reached a position where even the world's largest corporations dared not deny its influence if they wished to remain viable concerns during the 1980s.

In the space of only one decade, this tiny device has become a major part of everyday industrial, commercial, scientific and educational life. Its future existence is assured and the various societies of the world will have to become accustomed to it as a part of everyday life.

Information and communications

Possession of information has always been important to societies and to groups within societies. This was true for ancient times as well as for our own times. It affects all areas of life whether military, commerce, politics, social services, medicine or education. But simply gathering items of information is not enough. Once collected, the information has to be processed so that trends or totals or new knowledge can be extracted. These results have then to be passed on to those elected to handle them.

We have already seen in chapter 2 that the computer is pre-eminent in processing information. Computer centres linked together into **computer networks** can transfer processed information by telecommunications within seconds so that institutions in the network, located anywhere in the world, can access the same information.

Computer networks have existed between banks, universities and major world companies for the past decade. So where does the little microcomputer make its impact? Today anyone can have access to computing power through the microcomputer. It is cheap enough to be within the grasp of even small businesses, and compact enough to be easily confined in any office or home. In the coming decade they will become ubiquitous. But this accounts only for the processing power of the micro. There is still the other matter of the transmission of information on a large scale to individual microcomputer owners. Here we need reference to the rapid developments of telecommunications over the past years in the shape of satellite communications, optic fibres, viewdata systems, and the wandering or cordless telephone in order to appreciate that it will be a mere matter of time before networks between micro owners become commonplace. Indeed, at Imperial College, London, the Computer Centre can authorise owners of Research Machines to access information stored in its large central computer system from any part of the country. It is a two-way contact enabling information to be stored as well as retrieved. Similar networks exist at Hatfield in Hertfordshire and at Birmingham for local "Computing in Schools" projects so that any school with a microcomputer can access stored data files or programs from one of the centralised sources. In turn, the large computer centres can amass information and, when linked together, microcomputer users can access information held in any of the centres in the network. (See figure 8.1.)

Before too long, a researcher in Tokyo hearing of a research paper held, for example, in the British Library, will have the means to request a copy and within minutes be reading it at home or in the office. The impact of this combination of the processing power of the microcomputer and the transmission of information via telecommunications will be to convert our world into an *Information Society*. However, every major technological revolution in the past has had its own side effects, some good, some bad. A few of the issues resulting from the microelectronic revolution are discussed in the following pages.

Privacy of personal information

The passage of information of a research nature via computer networks to help individuals expand their own knowledge more quickly and easily is a positive advantage. Most of us, however, become touchy when information contains our own personal details. Today, certain information about individuals exists in many separate computer files and, if this trend continues, it will not be long before fairly comprehensive records on every person could exist in different filing systems, e.g. information about one's driving licence, criminal records, medical

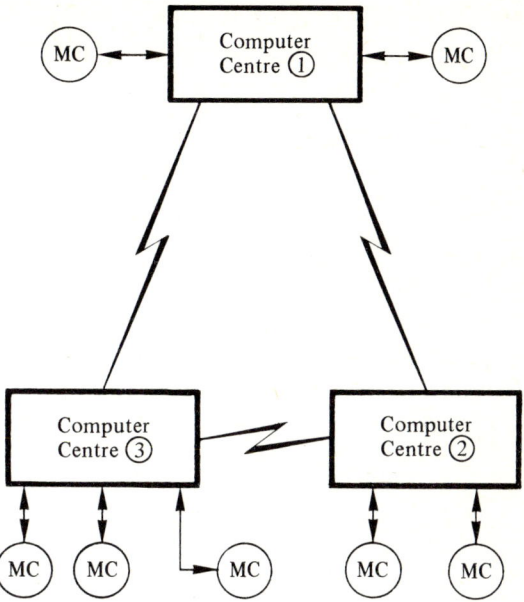

Figure 8.1 Each round node represents a microcomputer linked into a central computer system. The user has access to information stored in that system.

The larger centres, in the same country or in different parts of the world, are linked by telecommunications. Now each microcomputer user may have access to information stored in any one of these major centres.

records, social security payments, work records, tax records, credit ratings, mailing lists, shopping accounts, and even a complete school record from the age of five. Many of these already exist.

It would be a relatively easy matter for computer systems to be linked together so that these individual files could be combined into a complete life history for each person. With the use of universal personal identifiers, i.e. a unique personal number used on every form and record (already common in certain European countries), this correlation of information is child's play for the computer. Is this desirable? Should people be allowed to know what information is held about them on computer files? Should they be allowed to check the details and to report any errors? Who should be given authorisation to read personal files? How can the individual know who has read the file or whether misinterpreted information has been stored. These are just some of the issues being debated.

An example may help to illustrate current anxiety. In the USA in particular, credit rating systems are common. A substantial number of people have already had their reputations tarnished because incorrect data had been recorded about their credit worthiness. An even more terrifying situation is that an unscrupulous government could have access to all known information about any individual, even details about eating habits and the journals and magazines subscribed to. In a summary of the Data Protection Committee's report in 1978, Sir Norman Lindop, the chairman, said: "We did not fear that Orwell's 1984 was just around the corner, but we did feel that some pretty frightening developments could come about quite quickly and without most people being aware of what was happening."

An extension of such a development could be applied to CAL. Widespread use of CAL, in which the computer would generate lessons only on what is held in its storage system, could be used to brainwash youth into rigid social and philosophical patterns.

Employment or unemployment?

Another topical problem is that of microcomputers taking over our jobs. One extreme view sees the introduction of micros as a direct threat to 90% of the existing workforce with job losses occurring in the newspaper industry, assembly line work, mining, typing, and clerical work, resulting in 10% of the labour force paying exorbitant government and welfare taxes in order to keep the rest of the country in the manner to which they are currently accustomed. An opposing view is that microtechnology could well increase the number of jobs so that the pessimists of the first view have less to concern themselves about than they suppose. Certainly the prediction that the microcomputer industry is set to become the world's number one industry, ousting even the motor car and the oil industries from the top positions, provides a forceful argument. Already the giant IBM company stands at number seven in the world's largest companies, and the industry as a whole suffers from a lack of qualified staff rather than an excess.

It is now generally accepted even amongst the trade unions of the USA, Europe, and the UK that the microelectronic industry must continue to flourish and expand and that industrial societies cannot afford to ignore its influence if they are to become or remain economically viable. The forecast is that those companies not adapting to microelectronic technology will not survive into the 1990s.

Computers causing unemployment is no new cry. It was prevalent, albeit on a smaller scale, during the 1960s when computer centres were being established in many commercial companies. One large football pools operation, which has reduced its staff by half over the past few years as a result of computerisation, claims that with current labour costs they would be out of business were it not for automation.

Industrial nations are undergoing economic problems resulting in rising unemployment. But to lay the blame solely at the microelectronic industry is not sensible. It is true that microcomputers will present some measure of an employment problem, probably resulting in earlier retirement, shorter working weeks, retraining several times during normal working life. Certain classes of work will not be good future prospects, but many professions such as teaching, medicine and management will survive and, indeed, be helped by the introduction of microcomputers. Again, many trades such as plumbing, building, home maintenance, electrical installation are purely human activities and will remain so.

Those who suffer from a belief that the world owes them a living, possibly as a result of our over-emphasised Welfare State, may not do well in a microelectronic society. Those who have the gumption to go out and find work, learn new skills and adapt to a changing society will survive.

Breaking down barriers

Of all the barriers which divide the world, ignorance through non-accessibility to knowledge is the most severe. Until recently, there seemed no answer to this problem. The cure lay in an enormous educational programme, the cost of which would have been prohibitive. Computers can be used within education very successfully to teach individuals via special learning programs (computer assisted learning) and via future electronic learning aids such as the Texas Instruments "Speak and Spell".

Both the CAL-type programs, or *packages* as they are known, and the electronic learning aids are in their infancy. In electronic learning aids, voice output (also known as *speech synthesis*) is already commonplace. Add voice input and the developments of memory devices capable of holding many millions of binary data items, and these learning devices will proliferate. Already electronic dictionaries and phrase books are being developed which will easily be held in the businessman's briefcase or pocket. When produced by the millions they will become as cheap as the pocket calculator. Before long, electronic teaching books will be available. These books will not be the passive type such as the one you are now reading. They will encourage you to learn by asking you questions and commenting upon your replies. They will help you to revise some point not quite grasped or praise you for some mastery of a point, just like a personal tutor.

For this to happen, commercial organisations must become involved and this is just beginning to happen. A huge educational industry is about to be created with equally huge profits to be made, but vast capital investment for development, many thousands of man-hours and marketing expertise are required. As the provision of such educational devices as well as its dissemination becomes cheaper via microelectronics and more commonplace via telecommunications, as well as being more attractively packaged, their availability to the Third World will become more assured. This cannot happen overnight but it should gather pace during the early 1990s and gradually reduce the educational gulf between developed and developing nations.

Global transmission of information of all kinds will encourage lateral communications of the kind favoured by open societies. Its success depends upon cheap electronic information processing devices (microcomputers) as well as an infinite capacity for electronic data transmission. Thousands of satellites are to be launched into orbit by the Space Satellite programme over the next decade. Through these devices, person-to-person cordless radio and telephone communication will become the norm in open societies as will as global transmission of television. This must encourage the spread of lateral communication between people. Professor Stonier of Bradford University has argued that the critical point at which an inward looking society finds it difficult to maintain control of information is when 20% of the population have telephones.

In his book *The Mighty Micro*,* Christopher Evans has this to say: ". . . it is a characteristic of any race which involves exponential acceleration that the man who gets off first continually pulls away from his opponent. It is clear that we are facing a calamitous political stress-point. Whether the world survives through the 1980s may not be dependent upon conflicts in the Middle East, Africa or on the Sino-Soviet frontier, but on the political implications of advanced computer technology."

Apart from the capitalist/communist conflict and the question of closed/open societies, another interesting battle ensues between the USA and Japan. For the last thirty years, the USA has dominated the computer industry, particularly through the giant IBM company. Japan, however, has been fully conscious of the microelectronic industry for a number of years. With relatively few natural resources, its economic strength lies in its reliable export trade. The 1980s have been marked as the decade in which the design, marketing and sales of microcomputers and microelectronic-based products would come to fruition. To achieve this end,

* Published by Gollancz, 1979.

Japan invested billions of pounds in the attempt to capture a large part of the microelectronic market. Not only are they destined to become the world's number one computer nation but they have already demonstrated their superiority in a number of instances, both in the technology and its application.

Towards AD 2000

We are accustomed to using AD 2000 as a date into the far future, yet it is less than twenty years away. To conclude this chapter let us consider a few of the highly probable changes over these next two decades. It is not new to point towards a society so reliant upon electronics that it no longer has need for paper or metal money. Already the plastic credit card is replacing money and even cheques. Credit will be the all-important criterion for payment of goods. The credit facility has come a long way over the years so that a businessman flying into different countries and staying at a variety of hotels has no need to hand over any money at all. We shall all be using plastic-coated electronic cards for most purchases even down to a packet of chewing gum or a bottle of beer. One pilot scheme in Italy uses a card with units of currency on it. When a purchase is made, one or more units is removed until the card has no more left. Once retailers of all sizes are connected to centralised banking systems, then customers will need only to supply credit cards for instant deductions to be made from their accounts.

As for electronic mail, many companies already possess the required technology: a terminal at the sending end, a terminal at the receiving end, a computer system, and the ordinary public telephone system to transfer the message. How long will it be before we are all passing "letters" through our own domestic terminals? Video-screens attached to these new "telephones" will enable us to view the person at the other end, should we find this desirable.

Furthermore, we shall see at the very least a decline of the printed word. The seeds are here in the form of the IBA's Oracle and the BBC's Ceefax servives offering what can only be classed as electronic magazines. Prestel, the Post Office viewdata system, differs from the above two in that it provides a two-way communication of information. The television set acts as a receiver of information transferred via the telephone network and the operator can request any information required through such viewdata-based services. And in the future, nobody will need to go out shopping, simply call up the local store, view the goods (in colour and in three dimensions, of course), key in requirements, and enter a credit card through a special credit attachment. How long before the goods will be delivered by robot-controlled vans?

Many people will not need to travel to the office daily. They can spend their working time at home. Any message or discussion can take place through video-screens and the boss will be displayed on the screen while actually talking. If it is preferred, a fade button could be used to eliminate the display. There will be no problem in having to leave files at the office. With tiny chips storing millions of binary data, entire filing cabinets can be carried in a briefcase. A copy can be left at the office so that any amendments to one set of files can be instantly updated in the other set. Human psychology will play an important part in the extent to which any of us will want to stay at home to work.

However individual we want to be, we all require the company of other people to some degree. For children this aspect is even more necessary and the prospect of spending one's entire school life at home learning lessons via domestic terminals linked into the local school computer system may not be all that desirable, from either the student's or the parent's point of view.

Other wonders in the form of electronic gadgets and gimmicks will proliferate over the next ten years. The wandering telephone and the crashless vehicle are two. There will be devices of positive benefit to many handicapped people such as micro-controlled artificial limbs, heart pacemakers and devices which will read any form of type to the blind. Chips can even be embedded in the larynx to control speech. Health monitors will be worn on the wrist and its sensors will take the wearer's temperature and pulse rate, assess skin moisture, and analyse the surrounding atmosphere for viruses. Diabetics could read their own blood-sugar condition; people with weak hearts could read off their body stress and an alarm would sound when their hearts are being over-stressed.

Electronic devices installed in our homes will talk to us, reminding us when to restock the freezer, when the Sunday roast is ready, and so on. Motor cars will speak their controls, electronic doorbells will take messages from any caller if we are out or relay any message to them. But these are mere gadgets and gimmicks. The real impact lies in the processing and transmission of information. World problems are reaching a stage where the unaided human mind cannot cope adequately. We need help from machines which will help us "think". Much research has gone into the creation of "intelligent machines" but a great deal more is required. With the micro-chip becoming even more sophisicated, the possibility of creating thinking machines, the ultra-intelligent machine, is becoming more of a reality. If this appears somewhat far-fetched, it should be noted that some computer scientists are already calling for a halt into Artificial Intelligence. They feel that matters are going ahead too *quickly* and that society requires time to adjust to such concepts.

Biotechnology

As the world's natural resources become scarcer and oil prices continue to rise, there is increasing pressure for cheaper and more secure supplies of energy and chemicals. This is possible through the marriage of biotechnology and microtechnology, or the *bugs* and the *chips* as they have come to be known. The chip or the microprocessor processes information, the bug or biotechnology involves the processing of living cells.

A joint working party comprising the Advisory Council for Applied Research and Develop-

ment, the Advisory Board for the Research Council, and the Royal Society reported in March, 1980:

"We envisage biotechnology . . . creating wholly novel industries, with low fossil energy demands, which will be of key importance to the world economy in the next century.

We are convinced that it will shortly be possible to use microbial and other cells to make a wide range of organic chemicals which either cannot at present be made economically on a large scale or, if they can be made, require extensive inputs of land, energy and capital plant for their production from feedstocks, such as oil, which will become more expensive."

For this to happen there must be effective control over biological processes. It is here that microtechnology offers a cheap form of control which will help to reduce capital investment. At the moment, biotechnology has met with success in fermentation processes. For example, Japan leads the world in the production of certain chemicals, such as amino acids, microbial enzymes and antibiotics by fermentation processes. France, in its search for energy production from crops and agricultural and other organic wastes, has achieved a current output equivalent to two million tons of oil and hopes to increase this to ten million by AD 2000.

A more futuristic element of biotechnology is in the field called *bioelectronics*. One research team investigating electronic currents produced by plants under the stimulus of light is aiming to create artificial cell membranes which will perform in a similar way to natural plants. One practical application would be the creation of biological components performing basic computer functions such as memory storage. Even more fascinating is the possibility of linking the human brain to a computer system so that the output from the brain can be fed into the computer.

At present, the future of biotechnology in general is uncertain. But who knows what will develop over the next twenty years? What is certain is that the next two decades leading up to the year AD 2000 are going to be full of new developments.

Alexander Bell could hardly have foreseen a hundred years ago the changes in the reorganisation of society as a result of his invention of the telephone. A reorganisation of society on a similar if not a larger scale will have to take place with the impact of microelectronic technology on our society. This is why the education of our future citizens in microelectronic technology is a matter to be taken very seriously.

The microelectronic tide is coming in and very quickly. Tomorrow's technology is being demonstrated today, or, as someone has put it, science fact is catching up with science fiction.

We cannot stop the tide except an a temporary basis. We shall have to accept it. William Shakespeare, although in a different context, summed up the matter in the following delightful way:

"There is a tide in the affairs of men,
Which taken at the flood leads onto fortune,
Omitted, all the voyage of their life
is bound in shallows and in miseries.
On such a full sea are we now afloat,
And we must take the current when it serves,
Or lose our ventures."
(*Julius Caesar*, IV, 3, 217 – Brutus.)

Index